The Speed of Leadership

Dedication

This book is dedicated to David C.C. Dayton

"In the vast landscape of leadership, your influence has been undeniable. This book emerges not merely as a testament to your leadership style but as a response to the glaring need for a better example. May these pages serve as a subtle guide, bridging the gap between what is and what could be."

Introduction

In the dynamic realm of leadership, where change is constant and challenges are ever-evolving, there exists a transformative force – the Speed of Leadership. This concept encapsulates the essence of not just leading, but leading with purpose, agility, and impact. As we embark on this journey through the principles of the Speed of Leadership, prepare to unlock the keys that will propel you into the realm of exceptional leadership.

The Speed of Leadership isn't about racing through tasks or hastily making decisions. Instead, it's a strategic approach, a mindset that recognizes the need for adaptability, resilience, and a keen understanding of the ever-accelerating pace of the leadership landscape. To navigate this terrain successfully, we delve into ten fundamental tenets, each representing a crucial facet of leadership excellence.

By comprehending and embodying the principles laid out in each chapter, you are not merely learning to lead – you are learning to lead exceptionally. The Speed of Leadership is a guide, a mentor, and a catalyst for your leadership journey. As you absorb the insights within these pages, envision yourself evolving into a leader who not only navigates change but thrives within it.

In the spirit of learning from the best, each chapter unfolds with the wisdom of renowned leaders who have left an indelible mark on the world. Their words echo through time, resonating with the very principles we explore in the Speed of Leadership. These quotes serve as guiding beacons, illuminating the path to mastery in leadership.

As we embark on this odyssey together, remember that exceptional leadership is not a destination but a continuous journey of growth and adaptation. The Speed of Leadership is your compass, your companion, and your source of inspiration. Let the exploration begin.

Prologue

Trust

"If people like you, they'll listen to you, but if they trust you, they'll do business with you."

- Zig Ziglar

Building Trust

Building trust involves establishing a foundation of credibility and reliability. Leaders should authentically communicate their values, admit mistakes when necessary, and consistently follow through on commitments. A leader's openness about their own vulnerabilities can create a climate of trust, encouraging team members to reciprocate. Transparency builds a bridge between the leader and the team, fostering an environment where trust can flourish organically.

Establishing Credibility

Credibility is not just about showcasing expertise; it's about demonstrating a genuine commitment to continuous learning. Leaders should stay abreast of industry developments, invest time in honing their skills, and showcase a readiness to adapt. A leader's credibility is bolstered when team members perceive them as knowledgeable, reliable, and capable of navigating challenges with competence.

The Team Trust Dynamic

Trust within a team is a collective effort. It's about creating an atmosphere where team members feel safe to express their ideas and concerns. Leaders can facilitate trust by fostering a culture of mutual respect, acknowledging diverse perspectives, and ensuring everyone feels valued. When team members trust each other, collaboration becomes more innovative and productive.

Historical Perspectives

Examining historical leaders provides tangible examples of trust in action. Abraham Lincoln's leadership during the Civil War serves as a powerful illustration. His honesty and integrity not only earned him the trust of the nation but also empowered him to navigate a deeply divided country. Historical narratives offer valuable lessons on the enduring impact of trust in leadership.

The Dance of Trust and Speed

The challenge lies in synchronizing the need for swift decision-making with the patient cultivation of trust. Trust is a dynamic force that, once established, accelerates the speed of leadership. Leaders must navigate this delicate dance, knowing when to act decisively and when to invest time in relationship-building. Striking the right balance ensures that speed and trust amplify each other rather than working at cross-purposes.

In the chapters ahead, we will delve deeper into each of these components, unraveling the intricacies of trust in leadership and its dynamic interplay with the swift pace required at the helm. Trust is not merely a quality; it is the essence that propels leaders forward in the relentless pursuit of excellence.

Humility

"It takes 20 years to build a reputation and five minutes to ruin it. If you think about that, you'll do things differently."
- Warren Buffett

In the tapestry of leadership virtues, humility stands as a cornerstone, weaving a thread of authenticity and self-awareness. Warren Buffett's quote encapsulates the fragility of reputation, underscoring the importance of humility in every leader's journey. As we explore the second component of "The Speed of Leadership" — Humility — we unravel the layers of its impact on individuals, teams, and organizational success.

Understanding Humility

At its core, humility is not about self-deprecation or downplaying achievements; rather, it is the recognition that success is a collective effort. Leaders with humility acknowledge the contributions of others, embrace a continuous learning mindset, and approach challenges with an openness to new perspectives. It's an acknowledgment that leadership is a journey of growth and development, not a final destination of superiority.

The Power of Self-Awareness

Humility and self-awareness are inseparable companions. Leaders who understand their strengths and weaknesses create an environment where authenticity thrives. They seek feedback, admit mistakes, and view setbacks as opportunities for growth. This self-awareness not only fosters personal development but also engenders trust and respect among team members.

Building a Culture of Humility

Leaders set the tone for organizational culture, and humility can be a guiding force in shaping a healthy work environment. By celebrating the successes of the team and attributing achievements to collective efforts, leaders cultivate a culture where individuals feel valued. A humble leader fosters collaboration, creating a space where diverse talents flourish, and innovation thrives.

Humility in Decision-Making

The humility to acknowledge uncertainty and seek input from others is a hallmark of effective decision-making. Leaders who recognize the limitations of their knowledge and actively solicit diverse opinions make more informed choices. This approach not only enhances the quality of decisions but also reinforces the trust that team members place in their leader's judgment.

Lessons from Leaders

Historical figures offer profound lessons in humility. Mahatma Gandhi's commitment to serving others and his willingness to lead by example demonstrated a rare humility that inspired a nation. Examining such leaders provides tangible insights into the transformative power of humility in shaping destinies.

The Humble Leader's Legacy

The impact of humble leadership extends beyond the immediate horizon. Leaders who prioritize humility leave a lasting legacy, remembered not only for their accomplishments but for the way they empowered others. The humility-driven legacy is one where individuals are inspired to carry forward the torch of leadership, fostering a cycle of continuous improvement.

Balancing Confidence and Humility

Humility does not negate confidence; rather, it tempers it with a realistic understanding of one's place within a broader context. Leaders can be confident in their abilities while recognizing the contributions of others. This balance ensures that humility becomes a catalyst for collaboration and innovation, rather than a barrier to assertiveness.

The Journey Towards Humility

The journey towards humility is ongoing. It involves self-reflection, a commitment to learning, and a genuine desire to uplift others. Leaders who embrace this journey not only enrich their own lives but also create a ripple effect that transforms the entire organizational landscape.

In the chapters ahead, we will continue to explore the components of "The Speed of Leadership," each revealing a facet of leadership excellence. Humility, with its transformative power, invites leaders to navigate the path of self-discovery and collective growth, propelling teams forward at an accelerated pace.

Ethics

"The ultimate measure of a man is not where he stands in moments of comfort, but where he stands at times of challenge and controversy."

- Martin Luther King, Jr.

As we embark on the exploration of 'The Speed of Leadership,' the spotlight turns to Ethics — the moral compass that guides leaders through the complexities of decision-making and organizational conduct.

Defining Ethics in Leadership

At the heart of leadership lies the responsibility to make decisions that not only serve organizational goals but also align with a higher standard of morality. Ethics, in the leadership context, encompasses a set of principles that govern behavior, ensuring that actions are not only legal but also morally sound. It's the commitment to doing what is right, even when faced with challenging choices.

The Ripple Effect of Ethical Leadership

Ethical leadership extends beyond individual decisions; it shapes organizational culture and influences the behavior of the entire team. When leaders prioritize ethics, they set a standard that permeates through all levels of the organization. This commitment creates a positive ripple effect, fostering an environment where trust, integrity, and accountability flourish.

Ethical Decision-Making

Navigating the complex landscape of decision-making requires a keen understanding of ethical principles. Leaders must weigh the consequences of their choices not only in terms of immediate outcomes but also with an eye on the long-term impact. The process involves considering the interests of all stakeholders, fostering transparency, and upholding a commitment to fairness.

The Intersection of Trust and Ethics

Trust and ethics are intertwined facets of effective leadership. Trust is built on the foundation of ethical behavior, and ethical leaders earn the confidence of their teams. A leader's commitment to ethical conduct is a testament to their integrity, reinforcing the trust that team members place in their judgment. It becomes a reciprocal relationship — trust bolsters ethical leadership, and ethical leadership strengthens trust.

Lessons from Ethical Icons

History provides us with ethical icons whose leadership stood the test of time. Nelson Mandela, facing the crucible of apartheid, exhibited unwavering commitment to justice, reconciliation, and ethical leadership. Examining such examples not only inspires but also offers practical insights into the application of ethics in the face of adversity.

Navigating Ethical Gray Areas

Leaders often encounter situations where ethical principles seem to conflict, creating gray areas that require careful navigation. These moments demand a heightened ethical awareness, a commitment to seek guidance when needed, and the courage to make decisions that align with the core values of the organization. It's in these challenging times that the true mettle of ethical leadership is tested.

Embedding Ethics in Organizational DNA

Ethical leadership is not a mere checkbox; it's an ongoing commitment to embed ethical principles in the very DNA of the organization. This involves fostering a culture where ethical behavior is not just encouraged but expected. When ethics becomes an integral part of the organizational identity, it guides actions even in the absence of explicit rules.

The Price of Unethical Leadership

The consequences of unethical leadership are profound and far-reaching. Organizations led by leaders who prioritize short-term gains over ethical considerations risk erosion of trust, damaged reputation, and legal repercussions. The price of unethical leadership extends beyond immediate setbacks, leaving a lasting stain on the organizational legacy.

Building an Ethical Framework

Leaders can actively shape an ethical framework by establishing clear guidelines, providing ethics training, and fostering open communication. An ethical framework serves as a compass for the entire organization, offering guidance in moments of uncertainty and reinforcing the shared commitment to integrity.

The Dynamic Balance of Ethics and Speed

In the swift current of leadership, the challenge is to maintain ethical standards without compromising the pace of decision-making. Ethical leaders find a dynamic balance, recognizing that speed is not an excuse to bypass ethical considerations. It's a conscious effort to integrate ethical thinking into the speed of leadership, ensuring that every decision aligns with the moral compass of the organization.

In the upcoming chapters, we will continue our exploration, unraveling the intricacies of leadership excellence. Ethics, as a guiding force, invites leaders to navigate the complexities of decision-making with unwavering integrity, propelling teams forward on the path of sustainable success.

Chapter 1: Speed

"The speed of the leader determines the rate of the pack"
- Ralph Waldo Emerson

'The Speed of Leadership' invites us to delve into the intricate dance of swift decision-making, agile adaptation, and the pursuit of excellence at an accelerated pace. As we focus on 'Speed,' we explore not just the necessity of quick actions but the art of navigating velocity with precision.

The Imperative of Speed in Leadership

In a fast-evolving landscape, the ability to act swiftly is a distinguishing trait of effective leadership. Speed in decision-making is not just about urgency but also about agility — the capacity to adapt to changing circumstances. Leaders who harness the imperative of speed understand that it's not a race to recklessness but a calculated journey toward innovation and progress.

The Agility-Adaptation Nexus

Speed is not synonymous with haste. It's about being agile, possessing the capacity to pivot and adapt without sacrificing the quality of decisions. Agile leaders anticipate change, embrace uncertainty, and cultivate a culture where adaptation is not just tolerated but celebrated. The agility-adaptation nexus is the cornerstone of sustained success in a dynamic environment.

The Spectrum of Decision Speed

Leadership decisions exist on a spectrum of speed, from routine choices that benefit from rapid execution to strategic decisions that demand thorough contemplation. A nuanced understanding of this spectrum empowers leaders to discern when to accelerate and when to deliberate. The art lies in gauging the velocity required for optimal outcomes.

Technology as an Accelerator

In the digital era, technology serves as a potent accelerator of leadership speed. Harnessing technological tools for data analysis, communication, and collaboration enhances the efficiency of decision-making processes. However, the reliance on technology must be balanced with the human element — the intuition, empathy, and creativity that define effective leadership.

The Psychology of Speed

Understanding the psychology of speed is essential for leaders navigating the swift currents of decision-making. It involves managing the tension between urgency and thoughtfulness, recognizing that the perception of speed is as crucial as the actual pace. Leaders who cultivate a mindset that values both speed and thoroughness foster an environment where teams can perform at their best.

The Balancing Act

Speed in leadership is a delicate balancing act. It requires the discernment to distinguish between decisions that demand rapid execution and those that necessitate a more measured approach. Leaders must navigate the tension between speed and precision, recognizing that the pursuit of excellence does not tolerate the sacrifice of quality on the altar of expediency.

Learning from Speedsters

Examining leaders who mastered the art of speed provides valuable insights. Steve Jobs, renowned for his swift and bold decisions at Apple, demonstrated how speed, when harnessed with vision, can redefine industries. Learning from such speedsters involves dissecting not just their decisions but the mindset and strategies that propelled them forward.

Organizational Velocity

Beyond individual decision-making, organizational velocity defines the collective speed of a team. It involves optimizing processes, fostering a culture of innovation, and empowering team members to act autonomously when necessary. Leaders who cultivate organizational velocity create a dynamic ecosystem where the entire team moves cohesively toward shared goals.

Mitigating Risks in the Fast Lane

The speed of leadership is not without risks. Leaders must be vigilant in identifying and mitigating risks associated with swift decisions. This involves leveraging data-driven insights, encouraging diverse perspectives, and instituting mechanisms for continuous feedback. The goal is not to eliminate risk but to navigate it with a calculated approach that aligns with organizational objectives.

Ethical Considerations in Speed

While speed is imperative, ethical considerations must not be sacrificed in the pursuit of expediency. Leaders must infuse their swift decisions with a moral compass, ensuring that speed does not compromise integrity. The challenge lies in aligning the velocity of leadership with the ethical principles that define the character of the organization.

Nurturing a Speed-Ready Culture

Creating a speed-ready culture involves instilling a sense of urgency without inducing panic. It requires fostering an environment where innovation is encouraged, failure is viewed as a stepping stone to success, and continuous improvement is ingrained in the organizational DNA. A speed-ready culture empowers teams to embrace change and respond adeptly to evolving challenges.

The Art of Swift Communication

Effective leadership speed relies heavily on communication. Leaders must articulate their vision, decisions, and expectations with clarity and precision. The ability to convey complex ideas succinctly, inspire action, and provide timely feedback is a hallmark of leaders who master the art of swift communication. Communication becomes the conduit through which speed is translated into meaningful action.

The Paradox of Patient Speed

In the pursuit of speed, leaders must recognize the paradox of patient speed. It involves maintaining a sense of urgency while allowing the necessary time for thoughtful consideration. Leaders who embrace this paradox understand that not all decisions can or should be made in haste. Patient speed involves strategic patience — a deliberate and purposeful approach to decision-making.

Integrating Speed with Sustainability

The enduring success of leadership speed lies in its integration with sustainability. Swift decisions that sacrifice long-term sustainability for short-term gains can lead to unintended consequences. Leaders must consider the ripple effects of their choices, balancing the need for speed with a commitment to building a resilient and enduring organizational foundation.

Conclusion

In the symphony of leadership, speed is both a soloist and an ensemble player. It demands the skill to lead with velocity while orchestrating a harmonious collaboration of diverse talents. As we continue our journey through 'The Speed of Leadership,' let us recognize that the art lies not just in the swiftness of movement but in the precision, agility, and wisdom that define a leader's dance with speed.

Chapter 2: People

"No matter how brilliant your mind or strategy, if you're playing a solo game, you'll always lose out to a team."

- Reid Hoffman

As we continue to delve into the heart of 'The Speed of Leadership,' our focus turns to the fundamental essence of organizational dynamics — People. They are not merely the workforce; they are the architects of innovation, the driving force of success, and the soul of leadership.

The Human Element

Amidst the strategic frameworks and technological advancements, leaders must never lose sight of the human element. People are not mere resources but individuals with unique talents, aspirations, and potential. Effective leadership acknowledges this fundamental truth and recognizes that success hinges on nurturing, empowering, and valuing the people within the organization.

Empathy as a Leadership Virtue

At the core of exceptional leadership lies empathy — the ability to understand and resonate with the experiences, challenges, and triumphs of others. Leaders who cultivate empathy forge deep connections, building trust and loyalty within their teams. Empathy is not a sign of weakness; it is the cornerstone of compassionate and effective leadership.

Unleashing Human Potential

Leadership is not about commanding; it's about unlocking the vast reservoirs of human potential. Empowered and motivated individuals contribute exponentially to the collective success of the organization. Leaders who foster an environment of trust, encouragement, and continuous learning create a fertile ground where people can unleash their creativity and capabilities.

The Role of Leadership in Personal Growth

Beyond organizational goals, leaders bear a responsibility for the personal growth and development of their team members. This involves providing mentorship, constructive feedback, and opportunities for skill enhancement. A culture that values and invests in the growth of individuals not only enhances the capabilities of the team but also attracts and retains top talent.

Diversity as a Strength

The strength of a team lies in its diversity. Effective leaders embrace and celebrate individual differences, understanding that diverse perspectives lead to more innovative solutions. Inclusivity is not just a buzzword; it is a strategic imperative that propels organizations forward. Leaders who foster a culture of diversity create a resilient and adaptable workforce.

Building a Positive Organizational Culture

Organizational culture is the invisible hand that guides behavior and shapes the employee experience. Leaders play a pivotal role in shaping this culture. A positive culture, rooted in values, transparency, and respect, not only enhances employee satisfaction but also becomes a magnet for attracting like-minded individuals who align with the organizational ethos.

The Art of Motivation

Motivating a diverse group of individuals requires a nuanced understanding of what drives each person. Effective leaders tailor their motivational strategies, recognizing that what inspires one team member may not resonate with another. Whether through recognition, meaningful work, or professional development opportunities, motivation is the key to unlocking peak performance.

Navigating Challenges in Human Dynamics

Leadership is not immune to challenges in human dynamics. Conflicts, varying personalities, and communication breakdowns are inevitable. Exceptional leaders confront these challenges head-on, fostering open communication, mediating conflicts, and instilling a shared sense of purpose. The ability to navigate the complexities of human interactions is a hallmark of skilled leadership.

The Leader as a Servant

In the realm of 'People' in leadership, the concept of servant leadership emerges. Leaders who serve their teams, prioritize their well-being, and remove obstacles to success cultivate a culture of mutual respect and collaboration. The servant leader's focus is on empowering others, recognizing that the success of the team reflects the effectiveness of leadership.

Mentoring and Succession Planning

Leadership extends beyond the present moment; it involves preparing the next generation of leaders. Effective leaders engage in mentoring and succession planning, identifying high-potential individuals and providing them with the guidance and opportunities needed for future leadership roles. This forward-looking approach ensures the continuity of leadership excellence.

Handling Leadership Transitions

Leadership transitions are inevitable in the life of an organization. Whether due to promotions, retirements, or external changes, how leaders manage these transitions profoundly impacts the team and organizational continuity. Leaders who navigate transitions with transparency, clear communication, and a focus on stability minimize disruption and maintain momentum.

Wellness and Work-Life Integration

The well-being of people extends beyond the workplace. Leaders who prioritize employee wellness and advocate for work-life integration foster a healthier and more productive workforce. Recognizing the importance of a holistic approach to well-being, leaders create an environment where individuals can thrive both personally and professionally.

Listening as a Leadership Skill

Amidst the cacophony of challenges and opportunities, leaders must hone the skill of active listening. Understanding the concerns, ideas, and aspirations of team members requires a genuine commitment to listening. Leaders who listen foster an inclusive environment where every voice is heard, contributing to a culture of collaboration and innovation.

Celebrating Achievements

In the pursuit of organizational goals, it's essential to pause and celebrate achievements. Acknowledging the hard work and accomplishments of the team instills a sense of pride and reinforces a positive organizational culture. Leaders who take the time to celebrate not only boost morale but also create a motivated and engaged workforce.

Nurturing Trust

Trust is the bedrock of effective leadership. Building and maintaining trust requires consistency, transparency, and integrity. Leaders who prioritize trust create a foundation that sustains the team through challenges and uncertainties. Trust is not bestowed; it is earned through a demonstrated commitment to the well-being and success of the people entrusted to leadership.

Continuous Feedback and Performance Management

The traditional annual performance review is evolving into a continuous feedback model. Leaders who provide regular, constructive feedback empower individuals to course-correct, improve, and excel. The goal is not just performance evaluation but continuous development, aligning individual growth with organizational success.

Remote Leadership and Flexibility

In an era of remote work and virtual teams, leadership transcends physical boundaries. Leaders must adapt to new paradigms of collaboration, embracing technology and fostering a culture of flexibility. Remote leadership involves not just managing tasks but also understanding the unique challenges and opportunities presented by virtual work environments.

The Legacy of Leadership

A leader's impact extends far beyond their tenure. The legacy of leadership is measured not only by organizational achievements but by the enduring influence on the lives and careers of the people led. Leaders who leave a positive legacy inspire a culture of excellence that outlasts their time in leadership.

Conclusion

In the intricate mosaic of leadership, 'People' form the vibrant hues that give meaning and purpose to the entire canvas. As we navigate the complexities of 'The Speed of Leadership,' let us recognize that leadership is not a solitary journey but a collective dance, where the synergy of diverse talents, motivations, and aspirations propels organizations to unparalleled heights.

Chapter 3: Engagement

"Employees who believe that management is concerned about them as a whole person – not just an employee – are more productive, more satisfied, more fulfilled. Satisfied employees mean satisfied customers, which leads to profitability."

- Anne M. Mulcahy

Immersing ourselves in 'The Speed of Leadership,' we shift our focus to the pulsating heartbeat of organizational vitality — Engagement. It's not merely a buzzword; it's the dynamic force that propels teams forward, turning aspirations into achievements.

Defining Engagement

Engagement is more than a measure of job satisfaction; it's the emotional investment and commitment individuals bring to their work. It's a state where individuals are not just present but fully immersed in their roles, contributing their best to the shared goals of the organization. Engaged teams are the driving force behind innovation, productivity, and sustained success.

The Role of Leadership in Fostering Engagement

Engagement doesn't happen in a vacuum; it's cultivated and nurtured by effective leadership. Leaders who prioritize employee well-being, provide clear direction, and recognize individual contributions create an environment where engagement can thrive. The leader's role is not just to manage tasks but to inspire a sense of purpose and passion that propels the team forward.

Aligning Individual Goals with Organizational Vision

Engagement flourishes when individuals see a meaningful connection between their personal aspirations and the broader vision of the organization. Leaders play a crucial role in articulating this alignment, ensuring that each team member understands how their contributions contribute to the overarching goals. When personal and organizational objectives converge, engagement becomes a natural outcome.

Building a Culture of Recognition

Recognition is a powerful catalyst for engagement. Leaders who acknowledge and celebrate individual and collective achievements reinforce a positive feedback loop. It goes beyond formal rewards; sincere appreciation, whether public or private, fosters a sense of value and belonging. A culture of recognition transforms the workplace into a space where individuals feel seen, appreciated, and motivated.

Empowerment as a Driver of Engagement

Engagement is intricately linked to a sense of empowerment. Leaders who empower their teams by providing autonomy, entrusting responsibilities, and fostering a culture of innovation create conditions for high engagement. When individuals feel empowered to make a meaningful impact, they become more invested in the success of the organization.

Continuous Learning and Development

Engagement is not a static state; it thrives in an environment of continuous learning and development. Leaders who invest in the growth and skill enhancement of their teams not only enhance individual capabilities but also signal a commitment to the future. A culture of learning creates a dynamic atmosphere where engagement becomes a natural byproduct of personal and professional advancement.

Feedback as a Two-Way Street

The exchange of feedback is a cornerstone of engaged teams. Leaders who create a culture of open communication, where feedback flows in both directions, strengthen the bond between leadership and the team. Constructive feedback provides guidance for improvement, enhances performance, and reinforces the idea that each individual's voice is valued.

Wellness Programs and Work-Life Balance

Engagement extends beyond professional tasks; it encompasses the holistic well-being of individuals. Leaders who prioritize wellness programs and advocate for work-life balance create an environment where individuals can thrive both personally and professionally. A healthy work-life balance is not just a perk; it's a strategic investment in sustaining long-term engagement.

Inclusion and Diversity for Enhanced Engagement

Inclusive organizations, where diversity is not just acknowledged but celebrated, experience higher levels of engagement. Leaders who foster an inclusive culture create a sense of belonging for every team member. When individuals feel valued for their unique perspectives, backgrounds, and contributions, engagement becomes a shared commitment woven into the fabric of the organization.

Harnessing Technology for Virtual Engagement

In an era of remote work and virtual collaboration, leaders must leverage technology to facilitate engagement. Virtual team-building activities, digital communication tools, and platforms for shared accomplishments enhance the sense of connection among team members. Leaders who embrace technology as an enabler of engagement bridge geographical gaps and maintain a vibrant team spirit.

Purpose-Driven Leadership

Leadership with a clear sense of purpose resonates deeply with team members. When leaders articulate a compelling vision and align actions with a higher purpose, individuals connect with something beyond the day-to-day tasks. Purpose-driven leadership infuses the workplace with a sense of meaning, igniting a passion that fuels sustained engagement.

Flexibility and Adaptability in Leadership Styles

Effective leaders understand that engagement is not a one-size-fits-all proposition. Different individuals respond to varying leadership styles. Leaders who exhibit flexibility and adaptability in their approach, tailoring their leadership to the needs and preferences of each team member, foster a sense of understanding and connection that enhances overall engagement.

Team Building Beyond the Office

Team building is not confined to the office space. Leaders who invest in activities that foster camaraderie, whether in-person or virtual, build a strong foundation for engagement. Shared experiences, whether through team retreats, collaborative projects, or social events, strengthen the bonds among team members, creating a positive and connected workforce.

Succession Planning with Engagement in Mind

Engagement is intricately tied to the long-term success of the organization. Leaders who incorporate engagement considerations into succession planning ensure the continuity of an engaged and motivated leadership team. This forward-looking approach acknowledges that leadership transitions should not disrupt the positive momentum built through sustained engagement efforts.

The Emotional Connection

At the heart of engagement is the emotional connection individuals feel toward their work, colleagues, and the organization. Leaders who foster this emotional bond create an environment where individuals are not just employees but ambassadors of the organizational mission. The emotional connection transforms routine tasks into meaningful contributions, elevating the overall level of engagement.

Measuring and Adapting Engagement Strategies

Engagement is not static; it requires continuous measurement and adaptation. Leaders who employ surveys, feedback mechanisms, and key performance indicators to assess engagement levels can identify areas for improvement. The ability to adapt engagement strategies based on real-time feedback ensures that leadership remains responsive to the evolving needs and aspirations of the team.

Ethical Considerations in Engagement

Ethics plays a pivotal role in engagement. Leaders must ensure that engagement strategies are not manipulative or coercive. Authentic engagement is built on trust, transparency, and a genuine commitment to the well-being of individuals. Leaders who prioritize ethical considerations create an engagement framework that aligns with the values of the organization.

Conclusion

In the intricate dance of leadership, engagement is the rhythm that propels the entire ensemble forward. As we navigate 'The Speed of Leadership,' let us recognize that engagement is not a destination but a continuous journey. It's the collective heartbeat that transforms a group of individuals into a high-performing team, surging toward shared aspirations and achievements.

Chapter 4: Excellence

"Always deliver more than expected."

- Larry Page

As we traverse the terrain of 'The Speed of Leadership,' our focus intensifies on the transformative power of Excellence. It's not merely a goal; it's the unwavering commitment to continuous improvement and the relentless pursuit of the highest standards.

The Essence of Excellence

Excellence is not a one-time achievement; it's a mindset, a culture, and a way of being. At its core, Excellence demands a commitment to delivering the very best in every endeavor. It's about setting and surpassing standards, not just meeting expectations.

Leaders who embody the essence of Excellence inspire a culture where individuals strive for greatness in everything they do.

Leadership as the Standard-Bearer of Excellence

Leaders are the torchbearers of Excellence within an organization. Their actions, decisions, and expectations set the tone for the entire team. Exceptional leaders establish a precedent of Excellence by consistently modeling the behaviors and values they expect from others. In doing so, they create a culture where the pursuit of Excellence is ingrained in the organizational DNA.

Continuous Improvement and the Pursuit of Mastery

Excellence is not a static state; it's a journey of continuous improvement and the relentless pursuit of mastery. Leaders who foster a culture of continuous learning, adaptability, and innovation create an environment where individuals are empowered to enhance their skills and contribute to the collective pursuit of Excellence. The commitment to mastery propels the organization toward sustained success.

Setting High Standards

Leadership Excellence begins with setting high standards. It involves establishing clear expectations for quality, performance, and conduct. High standards serve as a catalyst for individual and team achievement, pushing everyone to exceed their perceived limitations. When leaders consistently uphold and communicate these standards, they create a culture where Excellence is not just an aspiration but an expectation.

Accountability and Responsibility

Excellence flourishes in an environment of accountability and responsibility. Leaders who instill a sense of ownership among team members create a culture where individuals take pride in their work and outcomes. Accountability fosters a commitment to delivering results, and responsible leadership ensures that each team member understands the significance of their role in achieving organizational Excellence.

Alignment of Values with Excellence

Values are the compass that guides the journey toward Excellence. Leaders who align organizational values with the pursuit of Excellence create a powerful synergy. When values reflect a commitment to integrity, collaboration, innovation, and customer focus, they become the guiding principles that steer the organization toward extraordinary achievements.

Innovation as a Driver of Excellence

Excellence thrives in an atmosphere of innovation. Leaders who encourage creativity, experimentation, and the exploration of new ideas foster a culture where individuals are not afraid to challenge the status quo. Innovation becomes a conduit for achieving Excellence, pushing the boundaries of what's possible and driving the organization toward new heights of success.

Embracing a Growth Mindset

A growth mindset is the cornerstone of individual and organizational Excellence. Leaders who cultivate a culture of continuous growth and learning foster an environment where challenges are viewed as opportunities for improvement. Embracing a growth mindset encourages resilience, adaptability, and a belief that every setback is a stepping stone toward greater Excellence.

Building a Team of Excellence

A team of Excellence is more than the sum of its parts; it's a collective force that elevates performance to extraordinary levels. Leaders who assemble and nurture teams with diverse talents, shared values, and a commitment to mutual support create a powerhouse of Excellence. A team that embraces the principles of Excellence becomes a dynamic force that propels the entire organization forward.

Recognition of Excellence

Celebrating and recognizing Excellence is a fundamental leadership practice. Leaders who acknowledge and reward outstanding achievements reinforce the importance of striving for Excellence. Recognition is not just about applauding success; it's about reinforcing the behaviors, values, and efforts that contribute to the culture of Excellence within the organization.

Quality as a Pillar of Excellence

Excellence and quality go hand in hand. Leaders who prioritize quality in products, services, and processes set the foundation for organizational Excellence. Quality is not just a checkbox; it's a commitment to delivering value, meeting or exceeding customer expectations, and building a reputation for Excellence that resonates in the marketplace.

Ethical Considerations in the Pursuit of Excellence

Excellence and ethics are intertwined facets of leadership. Leaders must ensure that the pursuit of Excellence is guided by ethical principles. Upholding integrity, transparency, and fairness is non-negotiable in the quest for Excellence. Leaders who navigate the path of Excellence with unwavering ethical standards build a legacy of trust and credibility.

Learning from Setbacks and Failures

In the journey toward Excellence, setbacks and failures are inevitable. Exceptional leaders view these moments not as roadblocks but as opportunities for learning and improvement. Leaders who foster a culture where individuals are not afraid to take calculated risks, learn from failures, and iterate on their approaches create an environment conducive to sustained Excellence.

Leadership Agility and Adaptation

Leadership agility and adaptation are critical elements in the pursuit of Excellence. In a rapidly changing landscape, leaders must be agile in navigating complexities, adapting strategies, and embracing innovation. Agility involves not only responding swiftly to external changes but also fostering a culture where the organization is proactive in anticipating shifts in the market, technology, and customer expectations.

Adaptable leaders recognize that the pursuit of Excellence requires a willingness to reassess, refine, and sometimes completely overhaul existing practices. They understand that clinging to the status quo can hinder progress. By encouraging a culture of continuous improvement and remaining open to change, leaders create an environment where the organization can evolve, staying ahead in the pursuit of Excellence.

The Customer-Centric Focus

Excellence is not solely an internal endeavor; it extends to the customer experience. Leaders who prioritize a customer-centric approach align organizational efforts with the goal of delivering exceptional value. Understanding and exceeding customer expectations become fundamental tenets of the pursuit of Excellence. Leaders who emphasize customer satisfaction create a loyal customer base, laying the foundation for sustained success.

Strategic Vision and Excellence

Leadership Excellence is inseparable from strategic vision. Leaders who possess a clear and compelling vision inspire others to strive for greatness. A well-defined strategy provides a roadmap for the organization, aligning efforts toward common goals. A strategic vision not only guides day-to-day decisions but also serves as a source of motivation, fueling the collective pursuit of Excellence.

Collaboration and Collective Excellence

Excellence is a collective effort that transcends individual achievements. Leaders who foster a collaborative culture, where team members share ideas, insights, and expertise, amplify the potential for Excellence. Collaborative environments harness the diverse strengths of the team, creating a synergy that propels the organization toward collective achievements that surpass individual capabilities.

Measuring and Celebrating Progress

In the pursuit of Excellence, measurement is essential. Leaders who establish key performance indicators (KPIs) and metrics aligned with organizational goals gain insights into progress. Regular assessments provide data to refine strategies and address areas for improvement. Additionally, celebrating milestones and achievements reinforces the commitment to Excellence, motivating the team to persist in their pursuit of greatness.

Legacy Building through Excellence

Leadership Excellence is not just about achieving short-term goals; it's about building a lasting legacy. Exceptional leaders understand that their impact goes beyond immediate successes. By instilling a culture of Excellence, nurturing talent, and making decisions with a long-term perspective, leaders create a legacy that extends far beyond their tenure, shaping the organization's trajectory for years to come.

Conclusion

In the grand tapestry of leadership, Excellence emerges as the masterpiece woven from the threads of vision, commitment, agility, collaboration, and an unwavering pursuit of the highest standards. As we navigate 'The Speed of Leadership,' let us recognize that Excellence is not a destination but a continuous journey. It's the commitment to surpassing yesterday's achievements, embracing innovation, and cultivating a culture where every individual contributes to the symphony of organizational greatness.

Chapter 5: Drive

"Let me tell you the secret that has led to my goal. My strength lies solely on my tenacity."

- Louis Pasteur

As we delve deeper, our focus intensifies on the transformative power of Drive. It's more than motivation; it's the relentless determination, passion, and resilience that propel leaders and teams toward the realization of ambitious goals.

The Essence of Drive

Drive is the inner fire that fuels action. It's the determination to overcome obstacles, the passion that ignites creativity, and the resilience that keeps leaders and teams pushing forward in the face of challenges. Leaders who embody the essence of Drive inspire a culture where individuals are not just motivated; they are driven by a deep sense of purpose and commitment.

Leadership as the Catalyst of Drive

Leaders are the catalysts of Drive within an organization. Their ability to articulate a compelling vision, set challenging goals, and create a sense of urgency cultivates the Drive that propels the team forward. Exceptional leaders understand that Drive is not imposed but cultivated by fostering an environment where individuals are empowered to connect their efforts to meaningful outcomes.

Passion as a Driving Force

Passion is the heartbeat of Drive. Leaders who ignite passion within themselves and their teams create a dynamic energy that propels the organization forward. Passion is not just enthusiasm; it's a deep emotional connection to the work, a commitment that transcends routine tasks, and a driving force that fuels sustained effort even in the face of adversity.

Setting Ambitious Goals

Drive thrives in the pursuit of ambitious goals. Leaders who set challenging and inspiring objectives create a sense of purpose that mobilizes the team. Ambitious goals not only propel the organization toward higher levels of performance but also challenge individuals to stretch beyond their comfort zones, unleashing the full potential of Drive.

Resilience in the Face of Challenges

Resilience is the backbone of Drive. In the journey toward ambitious goals, challenges are inevitable. Leaders who cultivate a resilient mindset within the team foster an environment where setbacks are viewed as opportunities for growth. Resilience enables individuals to bounce back from adversity, learn from experiences, and maintain the Drive to persist in the pursuit of excellence.

Creating a Sense of Urgency

Drive is amplified by a sense of urgency. Leaders who instill a collective understanding of the importance of timely action create an environment where individuals are driven by the awareness that every moment matters. Urgency fuels a proactive mindset, propelling the team to take decisive actions and make impactful contributions to the organization's objectives.

Motivation through Meaningful Work

Drive is sustained when individuals find meaning in their work. Leaders who connect tasks to a broader purpose, emphasizing the impact of individual contributions on organizational goals, inspire a sense of meaning that transcends routine responsibilities. Motivated by the understanding that their work matters, individuals channel their Drive into purposeful and impactful actions.

Adaptability and Drive

Drive is not rigid; it adapts to changing circumstances. Leaders who foster adaptability within the team empower individuals to recalibrate their efforts in response to evolving challenges. The ability to pivot without losing momentum ensures that Drive remains a dynamic force, steering the organization toward success in a rapidly changing landscape.

Learning from Setbacks and Failures

Setbacks are not deterrents to Drive; they are stepping stones to growth. Leaders who encourage a culture of learning from failures, viewing them as opportunities to refine strategies, fortify Drive within the team. Embracing setbacks as integral parts of the journey cultivates resilience, innovation, and a relentless commitment to Drive in the pursuit of organizational goals.

Drive as a Team Synergy

Drive is amplified in a collaborative environment. Leaders who foster a culture of teamwork, where individuals support and challenge each other, harness the collective power of Drive. Team synergy transforms individual determination into a formidable force that propels the entire organization forward, overcoming challenges and achieving shared objectives.

Recognition of Driven Efforts

Acknowledging and recognizing Driven efforts is a vital aspect of leadership. Leaders who celebrate the unwavering commitment, passion, and resilience of individuals reinforce the importance of Drive within the organizational culture. Recognition is not just about applauding achievements; it's about reinforcing the behaviors and values that contribute to a culture of relentless Drive.

Ethical Considerations in Driven Pursuits

Drive, when channeled ethically, becomes a force for positive change. Leaders must ensure that the pursuit of ambitious goals aligns with ethical principles. Upholding integrity, fairness, and transparency is essential in fostering a Drive that not only achieves extraordinary outcomes but does so in a manner consistent with the values of the organization.

Nurturing Intrinsic Motivation

Drive is most potent when it springs from intrinsic motivation. Leaders who tap into the individual aspirations, values, and passions of team members nurture a Drive that goes beyond external rewards. Intrinsic motivation creates a sustainable source of energy, ensuring that individuals remain committed to their pursuits even when external circumstances fluctuate.

Balancing Drive and Well-Being

While Drive propels individuals toward ambitious goals, leaders must also ensure a balance with well-being. Burnout can erode Drive, making it essential for leaders to foster an environment

41

that recognizes the importance of work-life balance. Leaders who prioritize the well-being of their team members, encourage breaks, and promote a healthy work environment ensure that Drive is sustainable and aligned with long-term success.

Empowering through Autonomy

Drive flourishes when individuals have a sense of autonomy and ownership. Leaders who empower team members by entrusting them with responsibilities, allowing them to make decisions, and fostering an environment of trust, amplify the Drive within the organization. Autonomy provides individuals with the agency to shape their roles, fostering a deeper commitment to achieving shared objectives.

Harnessing External Motivators

External motivators, such as recognition and rewards, can enhance Drive when used judiciously. Leaders who strategically employ external motivators align them with organizational goals, ensuring that they reinforce a culture of Drive rather than overshadow intrinsic motivations. Well-crafted incentive systems can serve as catalysts, boosting morale and propelling the team toward exceptional achievements.

Drive in the Face of Success

Success can either dampen or invigorate Drive, depending on how it's perceived. Exceptional leaders ensure that success becomes a stepping stone to greater aspirations. By setting new challenges and maintaining a mindset of continuous improvement, leaders prevent complacency and sustain the Drive that propels the organization toward ongoing success.

Leadership Agility in Driven Pursuits

Drive requires leadership agility. In the pursuit of ambitious goals, leaders must navigate changing landscapes, adapt strategies, and remain responsive to emerging opportunities. Agility ensures that Drive is not confined to a rigid plan but remains dynamic, enabling the organization to seize unforeseen possibilities and stay on course toward its objectives.

Commitment to Lifelong Learning

Drive is intertwined with a commitment to lifelong learning. Leaders who cultivate a culture of continuous growth, curiosity, and exploration foster an environment where individuals are driven by a thirst for knowledge. A commitment to learning ensures that Drive is not solely based on existing competencies but is continually fueled by the acquisition of new insights and skills.

Drive as a Catalyst for Innovation

Innovation and Drive are inseparable companions. Leaders who foster a culture of innovation create an environment where individuals are driven to explore novel solutions, challenge conventions, and push the boundaries of what's possible. Drive becomes the catalyst that propels the organization into uncharted territories, fostering a culture of adaptability and forward-thinking.

Leveraging Diversity in Driven Pursuits

Diversity amplifies Drive by bringing a spectrum of perspectives, experiences, and ideas to the table. Leaders who embrace diversity and inclusion create a vibrant environment where Drive is fueled by the richness of varied insights. Leveraging diverse talents ensures that the organization approaches challenges with a multitude of perspectives, enhancing problem-solving and driving innovative solutions.

Global Perspectives in Driven Leadership

In an interconnected world, leaders must adopt global perspectives in their pursuit of excellence. Drive extends beyond local boundaries, and leaders who understand and appreciate diverse global contexts enhance the organization's ability to navigate complexities. Global perspectives in leadership ensure that Drive is aligned with the realities of a dynamic and interconnected business landscape.

Sustainable Drive for Long-Term Impact

Sustainable Drive is the hallmark of leadership with enduring impact. Leaders who foster a culture where Drive is not solely tied to short-term objectives but is part of a larger, purpose-driven vision ensure that the organization's efforts have a lasting imprint. Sustainable Drive propels the organization toward long-term success, creating a legacy of resilience, passion, and unyielding commitment.

Conclusion

In the relentless journey of leadership, Drive emerges as the dynamic force that propels aspirations into reality. As we traverse 'The Speed of Leadership,' let us recognize that Drive is not just a motivator; it's the unwavering determination, passion, and resilience that transform challenges into opportunities and aspirations into achievements.

Chapter 6: Leadership

"The only safe ship in a storm is leadership."

- Faye Wattleton

Leadership is more than a role; it's a transformative force that shapes cultures, inspires individuals, and propels organizations toward enduring success.

The Essence of Leadership

Leadership transcends titles; it's a call to action and a commitment to guide others toward a shared vision. The essence of leadership lies in the ability to inspire, influence, and empower individuals to achieve collective goals. Exceptional leaders understand that leadership is not about authority but about fostering an environment where everyone can contribute their best to the organization.

Visionary Leadership

At the core of leadership is a clear and compelling vision. Visionary leaders articulate a future state that inspires and motivates the team. A well-defined vision provides direction, aligns efforts, and serves as a beacon that guides decision-making. Visionary leadership sparks a shared sense of purpose, igniting the Drive and commitment needed to navigate the complexities of 'The Speed of Leadership.'

Leading by Example

Leadership is not a spectator sport; it demands active participation. Leading by example is a fundamental practice that builds trust and credibility. Leaders who embody the values and behaviors they expect from others create a culture of authenticity. Actions speak louder than words, and exemplary leadership sets the standard for the entire organization.

Influential Leadership

Influence is the currency of effective leadership. Leaders who understand the power of influence recognize that it's not about coercion but about inspiring others to willingly follow a shared vision. Influential leadership leverages communication, emotional intelligence, and a deep understanding of individual motivations to cultivate a culture where collaboration and commitment thrive.

Adaptive Leadership in a Changing Landscape

In the dynamic landscape of 'The Speed of Leadership,' adaptability is a key attribute. Leaders must be agile in responding to change, embracing innovation, and navigating uncertainties. Adaptive leadership involves recognizing emerging trends, adjusting strategies, and inspiring a culture that views change as an opportunity for growth.

Servant Leadership

Servant leadership transcends self-interest; it prioritizes the well-being of others. Leaders who adopt a servant leadership approach focus on supporting, empowering, and enabling the success of their team members. The servant leader sees leadership as a responsibility to serve others, creating a culture of mutual respect, collaboration, and shared success.

Emotional Intelligence in Leadership

Emotional intelligence is the bedrock of effective leadership. Leaders who understand and navigate their own emotions while empathetically connecting with the emotions of others build strong interpersonal relationships. Emotional intelligence fosters a culture of trust, open communication, and collaboration, creating an environment where individuals feel valued and understood.

Strategic Leadership

Leadership is inherently strategic. Strategic leaders align organizational objectives with a clear roadmap, leveraging resources to achieve long-term success. Strategic leadership involves anticipating challenges, identifying opportunities, and making decisions that position the organization for sustained excellence. It's about not just navigating the present but sculpting the future.

Inclusive Leadership

Inclusivity is the hallmark of modern leadership. Inclusive leaders embrace diversity, recognizing that varied perspectives contribute to innovation and resilience. Inclusive leadership fosters an environment where every voice is heard, every contribution is valued, and individuals feel a sense of belonging. It's about creating a tapestry of talents that enriches the organizational landscape.

Responsible Leadership

Leadership comes with a profound responsibility. Responsible leaders consider the ethical, social, and environmental impact of their decisions. They lead with integrity, transparency, and a commitment to corporate social responsibility. Responsible leadership not only fosters trust but also ensures the organization operates as a positive force in the broader community.

Collaborative Leadership

In the interconnected world of contemporary leadership, collaboration is imperative. Collaborative leaders break down silos, encourage cross-functional teamwork, and leverage collective intelligence. Collaboration extends beyond internal teams to partnerships with external stakeholders, creating a network of support that enhances the organization's capabilities and impact.

Courageous Leadership

Leadership demands courage — the courage to make difficult decisions, confront challenges, and champion change. Courageous leaders inspire confidence and resilience in the face of adversity. They navigate uncharted territories with conviction, setting the tone for the organization to embrace risks, learn from failures, and pursue innovation fearlessly.

Developing Future Leaders

A key responsibility of leaders is to nurture the next generation. Developing future leaders involves mentorship, coaching, and creating opportunities for growth. Leaders who invest in the development of their team members ensure a legacy of leadership excellence, fostering a culture where leadership is a shared responsibility woven into the organizational fabric.

Communicative Leadership

Effective communication is the lifeblood of leadership. Communicative leaders articulate a clear vision, provide context for decisions, and foster open dialogue. Communication goes beyond words; it involves active listening, empathy, and the ability to convey a compelling narrative that resonates with the hearts and minds of the team.

Resilient Leadership in Adversity

Resilient leadership shines brightest in challenging times. Leaders who exhibit resilience remain steadfast in their commitment to the organization's goals, inspire hope, and guide the team through turbulent waters. Resilient leadership involves learning from setbacks, adapting strategies, and maintaining a focus on long-term objectives even in the face of adversity.

Sustainable Leadership Practices

Leadership is a marathon, not a sprint. Sustainable leadership practices prioritize the well-being of leaders themselves. Leaders who maintain a balance between professional and personal life, prioritize self-care, and continuously invest in their own development ensure that their leadership remains vibrant and impactful over the long haul.

Conclusion

In the grand narrative of 'The Speed of Leadership,' Leadership stands as the epicenter — the force that shapes culture, drives innovation, and propels organizations toward enduring success. As we embrace the multifaceted dimensions of leadership, let us recognize that it's not just a role or a set of skills; it's a transformative journey that requires continuous learning, adaptability, and a deep commitment to the well-being of individuals and the organization.

Chapter 7: Encouragement

"It always seems impossible until it's done."

- Nelson Mandela

Encouragement is the art of fostering a positive environment where each note contributes to the harmonious success of the entire ensemble.

The Essence of Encouragement

Encouragement is the catalyst that transforms challenges into opportunities and setbacks into stepping stones. At its core, it's the deliberate act of instilling confidence, motivation, and a sense of capability in others. Exceptional leaders understand that encouragement is not just a reaction to success; it's a proactive force that fuels continuous improvement and strengthens the fabric of the organizational culture.

Positive Reinforcement

Encouragement thrives on positive reinforcement. Leaders who acknowledge and celebrate individual and team achievements create a culture where effort is recognized and valued. Positive reinforcement goes beyond formal recognition; it involves expressing appreciation, providing constructive feedback, and reinforcing the connection between actions and positive outcomes.

Constructive Feedback as Encouragement

Constructive feedback is a powerful tool for encouragement. Leaders who offer feedback with a focus on improvement, growth, and development foster an environment where individuals feel supported in their journey. Constructive feedback is not about criticism but about guiding individuals toward enhanced performance and reinforcing their potential for future success.

Recognition of Effort

Encouragement extends to the acknowledgment of effort, not just outcomes. Leaders who recognize and appreciate the hard work, dedication, and perseverance of individuals create a culture where every step toward a goal is valued. Recognizing effort encourages a mindset of continuous improvement, where individuals feel motivated to invest their best in each endeavor.

Cultivating a Growth Mindset

Encouragement is closely linked to a growth mindset. Leaders who cultivate a culture where challenges are viewed as opportunities to learn and grow instill a mindset of continuous improvement. Encouraging a growth mindset fosters resilience, adaptability, and a belief that with effort and perseverance, individuals can overcome obstacles and achieve their goals.

Encouragement in Times of Challenge

True leadership is revealed in times of challenge. Leaders who offer encouragement during difficult periods inspire confidence and foster resilience. Encouragement in adversity involves acknowledging the challenges, providing support, and instilling a belief that, together, the team can overcome obstacles. It's a reminder that challenges are temporary, but the strength forged in adversity endures.

Inspiring a Positive Culture

Encouragement contributes to the creation of a positive organizational culture. Leaders who consistently inspire a positive atmosphere through words, actions, and attitudes foster an environment where individuals feel motivated and optimistic. A positive culture becomes a breeding ground for creativity, collaboration, and the collective pursuit of excellence.

Individualized Encouragement

Effective encouragement recognizes the uniqueness of individuals. Leaders who tailor their encouragement to the preferences, strengths, and aspirations of team members create a personalized experience. Individualized encouragement goes beyond generic praise; it resonates on a personal level, making individuals feel seen, valued, and understood.

Encouraging Collaboration

Encouragement is a potent force in fostering collaboration. Leaders who promote a collaborative spirit, appreciate team contributions, and recognize the synergy of collective efforts fuel a culture where individuals feel encouraged to collaborate openly.

Encouraging collaboration enhances team dynamics, creativity, and the ability to tackle complex challenges together.

Celebrating Milestones

Encouragement finds expression in the celebration of milestones. Leaders who acknowledge and celebrate both individual and collective achievements create a culture where success is not just a destination but a series of meaningful milestones along the journey. Celebrating milestones reinforces a sense of progress, instilling motivation for the next set of goals.

Encouraging Innovation and Creativity

Innovation flourishes in an environment of encouragement. Leaders who foster a culture that encourages innovative thinking, experimentation, and the sharing of creative ideas create a dynamic space for growth. Encouraging innovation involves recognizing and rewarding creative efforts, inspiring individuals to explore new possibilities and contribute fresh perspectives.

Encouragement as a Form of Support

Supportive leadership is inherently linked to encouragement. Leaders who offer support, guidance, and a helping hand create a foundation where individuals feel encouraged to take risks and pursue ambitious goals. Encouragement as support involves removing barriers, providing resources, and ensuring that individuals know they have the backing of leadership.

Encouragement Across Diverse Teams

Encouragement transcends cultural and diversity boundaries. Leaders who understand and respect the diverse backgrounds, perspectives, and communication styles of team members can tailor their encouragement to resonate with the entire spectrum of the team. Encouraging diversity not only strengthens team cohesion but also amplifies the richness of ideas and solutions.

Encouraging a Healthy Work-Life Balance

Encouragement extends to promoting a healthy work-life balance. Leaders who prioritize the well-being of their team members, acknowledge the importance of rest and rejuvenation, and discourage excessive work hours contribute to a culture where individuals feel valued not just for their productivity but for their overall well-being.

Encouraging Learning and Development

Encouragement is a driving force in promoting continuous learning and development. Leaders who actively support and encourage ongoing skill enhancement create an environment where individuals feel motivated to invest in their personal and professional growth. Encouraging learning fosters a culture of adaptability and ensures that the team remains at the forefront of industry advancements.

Encouragement Through Communication

Effective communication is a vessel for encouragement. Leaders who communicate with clarity, transparency, and empathy convey a sense of trust and encouragement. Encouragement through communication involves not only conveying positive messages but also actively listening, understanding concerns, and addressing challenges collaboratively.

Ethical Considerations in Encouragement

Encouragement must be guided by ethical considerations. Leaders must ensure that their encouragement aligns with the values and principles of the organization. Ethical encouragement involves promoting behaviors that contribute to the overall well-being of individuals and the organization, fostering an environment of fairness, respect, and integrity.

Encouragement in Times of Change

Change often brings uncertainty, and encouragement becomes a stabilizing force. Leaders who offer encouragement during times of change reassure individuals, provide clarity on the path forward, and instill confidence in their ability to adapt. Encouragement in times of change involves emphasizing the opportunities that come with change and highlighting the collective strength of the team.

Encouraging Feedback and Open Communication

Encouragement thrives in an environment of open communication. Leaders who actively encourage feedback, both positive and constructive, create a culture of continuous improvement. Encouraging open communication involves fostering an atmosphere where individuals feel comfortable sharing their thoughts, ideas, and concerns, contributing to a collaborative and transparent organizational culture.

Encouraging a Sense of Belonging

Encouragement extends to creating a sense of belonging within the organization. Leaders who emphasize inclusivity, appreciate diversity, and actively work to create a welcoming environment foster a culture where individuals feel valued and included. Encouraging a sense of belonging enhances team cohesion, engagement, and the collective pursuit of shared goals.

Encouragement as a Leadership Legacy

Leadership is not only about the present; it's about leaving a lasting legacy. Leaders who prioritize encouragement as a foundational element of their leadership style contribute to a legacy of positivity, resilience, and empowerment. Encouragement as a leadership legacy ensures that the organizational culture continues to thrive long after individual leaders have moved on.

Encouragement in Leadership Development

Leadership development is a journey, and encouragement is a guiding companion. Leaders who actively encourage aspiring leaders, provide mentorship, and create opportunities for leadership growth contribute to a robust leadership pipeline. Encouragement in leadership development involves instilling confidence, offering guidance, and fostering a mindset of continuous learning.

Sustainable Encouragement Practices

Encouragement is not a one-time effort; it requires sustainable practices. Leaders who consistently integrate encouragement into their leadership style, making it a part of everyday interactions, contribute to a positive and resilient organizational culture. Sustainable encouragement practices involve weaving encouragement into the fabric of leadership, ensuring its enduring impact.

Conclusion

As we reflect on the profound influence of Encouragement in 'The Speed of Leadership,' let us recognize its transformative power to uplift, inspire, and empower. In a world of constant flux, encouragement becomes the steady heartbeat that fuels individuals and teams, propelling them toward shared aspirations and enduring success.

Chapter 8: Adaptability

"You have to be very nimble and very open minded. Your success is going to be very dependent on how you adapt."

- Jeremy Stoppelman

Now, our focus shifts to the transformative power of Adaptability. It's not just a response to change; it's the proactive art of navigating uncertainty, embracing opportunities, and leading with agility in an ever-evolving landscape.

The Essence of Adaptability

Adaptability is the cornerstone of effective leadership in a world characterized by constant change. It's the capacity to adjust, evolve, and thrive amid dynamic circumstances. Exceptional leaders understand that adaptability is not merely a survival skill; it's a strategic advantage that allows organizations to stay ahead, seize opportunities, and respond resiliently to challenges.

Embracing Change as an Opportunity

Adaptability involves viewing change not as a threat but as an opportunity for growth. Leaders who instill a mindset that welcomes change foster a culture where individuals are open to new ideas, willing to experiment, and capable of pivoting when necessary. Embracing change as an opportunity creates an environment that thrives on innovation and continuous improvement.

Agile Decision-Making

Adaptability is reflected in agile decision-making. Leaders who make decisions with speed, flexibility, and a focus on the organization's strategic goals navigate uncertainties effectively. Agile decision-making involves gathering relevant information swiftly, involving key stakeholders, and being willing to adjust strategies based on evolving circumstances. It's about making informed choices in the face of ambiguity.

Flexibility in Leadership Style

Adaptability extends to leadership styles. Leaders who recognize the need for flexibility in their approach tailor their leadership style to the specific needs of situations and individuals. Flexibility in leadership involves adjusting communication methods, motivational techniques, and decision-making processes to align with the dynamic nature of challenges and opportunities.

Anticipating Change and Trends

Adaptability is heightened by the ability to anticipate change and emerging trends. Leaders who stay attuned to industry shifts, technological advancements, and socio-economic developments are better positioned to lead proactively. Anticipating change involves continuous monitoring, scenario planning, and fostering a culture where individuals are encouraged to contribute insights about potential future changes.

Resilience in the Face of Setbacks

Adaptability and resilience are intertwined. Leaders who cultivate resilience within the team create an environment where setbacks are viewed as temporary obstacles, not insurmountable barriers. Resilience involves learning from failures, maintaining a positive outlook, and bouncing back from challenges with renewed determination. It's the backbone that sustains adaptability in the face of adversity.

Iterative Problem-Solving

Adaptability is manifested in iterative problem-solving approaches. Leaders who encourage a culture of experimentation, iteration, and continuous learning empower individuals to find creative solutions. Iterative problem-solving involves testing hypotheses, learning from outcomes, and refining strategies based on real-time feedback. It's an adaptive and dynamic approach to addressing complex challenges.

Collaborative Adaptation

Adaptability thrives in a collaborative environment. Leaders who foster a culture of teamwork and collective problem-solving harness the diverse strengths of the team. Collaborative adaptation involves involving team members in the decision-making process, leveraging their varied perspectives, and collectively adjusting strategies to align with changing circumstances.

Technology Integration

In the digital age, adaptability includes the strategic integration of technology. Leaders who embrace technological advancements and guide their teams in leveraging digital tools position the organization for efficiency and innovation. Technology integration involves staying informed about emerging technologies, assessing their relevance, and integrating them strategically to enhance processes and outcomes.

Continuous Learning Culture

Adaptability is sustained through a continuous learning culture. Leaders who prioritize learning and encourage a thirst for knowledge within the team foster adaptability. A continuous learning culture involves providing opportunities for professional development, supporting skill acquisition, and recognizing the value of a knowledgeable and adaptable workforce.

Adapting Communication Strategies

Effective communication is a key element of adaptability. Leaders who tailor their communication strategies to different audiences, channels, and contexts enhance organizational agility. Adapting communication involves recognizing diverse communication styles, leveraging various platforms, and ensuring that messages are clear and resonant in the midst of change.

Agility in Strategic Planning

Adaptability permeates strategic planning. Leaders who approach strategic planning with agility anticipate shifts in the business landscape, adjust goals based on evolving priorities, and remain flexible in the execution of strategies. Agility in strategic planning involves a continuous reassessment of objectives, alignment with emerging opportunities, and responsiveness to market dynamics.

Cross-Functional Collaboration

Adaptability is amplified through cross-functional collaboration. Leaders who break down silos, encourage collaboration between different departments, and create cross-functional teams enhance organizational adaptability. Cross-functional collaboration involves sharing expertise, fostering a holistic understanding of organizational challenges, and collectively developing adaptive strategies that consider multiple perspectives.

Balancing Stability and Innovation

Adaptability involves striking a balance between stability and innovation. Leaders who maintain core stability while encouraging innovation create a dynamic equilibrium. Balancing stability and innovation involves preserving foundational elements that contribute to organizational strength while simultaneously fostering a culture that welcomes experimentation and evolution.

Embracing Diversity of Thought

Adaptability is enriched by embracing diversity of thought. Leaders who value diverse perspectives, backgrounds, and experiences within the team promote adaptability. Embracing diversity of thought involves recognizing that unique viewpoints contribute to robust decision-making, innovative problem-solving, and a more adaptable organizational culture.

Ethical Considerations in Adaptability

Adaptability must align with ethical considerations. Leaders ensure that adaptive strategies uphold ethical principles, safeguarding the organization's reputation and integrity. Ethical considerations in adaptability involve making decisions that balance the need for change with the ethical responsibilities towards stakeholders and the broader community.

Adaptive Leadership in Crisis

True adaptive leadership shines in times of crisis. Leaders who remain calm, make timely decisions, and guide the team through challenging periods exemplify adaptive leadership. Adaptive leadership in crisis involves a combination of resilience, strategic thinking, and the ability to inspire confidence, ensuring that the organization navigates crises with agility and emerges stronger on the other side.

Sustainable Adaptability Practices

Adaptability is not a one-time effort; it requires sustainable practices. Leaders who foster a mindset of continuous adaptation, integrate adaptive practices into the organizational culture, and prioritize the development of adaptive capabilities contribute to long-term success. Sustainable adaptability practices involve weaving adaptability into the fabric of leadership, ensuring its enduring impact in the face of evolving challenges.

Conclusion

As we embrace the dynamic nature of 'The Speed of Leadership,' Adaptability emerges as the choreography that allows leaders and organizations to dance gracefully amid change and uncertainty. In a world where the only constant is change, the ability to adapt becomes not just a skill but a strategic imperative for navigating the complexities of leadership and steering the organization toward sustained success.

Chapter 9: Diversity

"Diversity: the art of thinking independently together."

- Malcolm Forbes

Continuing our journey through 'The Speed of Leadership,' our focus expands to the transformative power of Diversity. It's not just an organizational imperative; it's a driving force that propels innovation, fosters resilience, and shapes a culture of belonging.

The Essence of Diversity

Diversity is more than a checkbox; it's the acknowledgment that every individual brings a unique set of experiences, backgrounds, and perspectives to the table. Exceptional leaders understand that diversity goes beyond visible differences; it encompasses diverse thoughts, approaches, and talents. The essence of diversity lies in creating an environment where every voice is not only heard but valued.

Inclusive Leadership

Diversity thrives under the umbrella of inclusive leadership. Leaders who actively foster inclusivity create a culture where individuals feel a sense of belonging, regardless of their differences. Inclusive leadership involves recognizing and embracing diversity, ensuring that every team member feels respected, valued, and empowered to contribute their best.

Embracing Diversity of Backgrounds

Diversity of backgrounds is a cornerstone of organizational strength. Leaders who appreciate and leverage the varied cultural, educational, and experiential backgrounds of their team members create a dynamic and innovative environment. Embracing diversity of backgrounds involves recognizing that unique perspectives enrich decision-making, problem-solving, and creativity.

Valuing Diversity of Thought

True diversity extends to diversity of thought. Leaders who actively seek out and value diverse perspectives foster a culture where individuals feel encouraged to express their unique ideas. Valuing diversity of thought involves creating an environment where individuals are not only permitted but encouraged to challenge assumptions, question norms, and contribute innovative solutions.

Breaking Down Biases

Diversity efforts must confront and dismantle biases. Leaders who actively address unconscious biases, stereotypes, and discriminatory practices contribute to creating a more inclusive and equitable workplace. Breaking down biases involves fostering awareness, providing education, and implementing policies that mitigate the impact of biases on hiring, promotion, and day-to-day interactions.

Gender Diversity and Equality

Gender diversity is a vital component of organizational success. Leaders who champion gender equality create a workplace where individuals, regardless of gender, have equal opportunities for growth and advancement. Gender diversity and equality involve ensuring that policies, practices, and organizational culture promote fairness and inclusivity, creating a level playing field for all.

Diversity in Leadership

Leadership is more impactful when it reflects the diversity of the workforce. Leaders who actively promote and support diversity in leadership positions set an example for the entire organization. Diversity in leadership involves cultivating a pipeline of diverse talent, providing mentorship opportunities, and actively addressing barriers that may hinder underrepresented individuals from ascending to leadership roles.

Ethnic and Cultural Diversity

The richness of ethnic and cultural diversity contributes to organizational vibrancy. Leaders who embrace and celebrate different cultural perspectives foster an environment where individuals feel proud of their heritage and bring their authentic selves to work. Ethnic and cultural diversity involves creating spaces for cultural celebrations, acknowledging diverse holidays, and promoting an inclusive atmosphere.

Neurodiversity

Neurodiversity recognizes and values differences in neurological functioning. Leaders who embrace neurodiversity create an environment where individuals with diverse cognitive abilities contribute uniquely to the organization. Supporting neurodiversity involves adapting workplace practices, providing accommodations, and promoting an inclusive culture that values the strengths of individuals with diverse neurotypes.

Diversity in Age and Experience

Age and experience diversity contribute to a well-rounded organizational culture. Leaders who recognize the value of diverse age groups and experiences within the team create a dynamic workplace. Diversity in age and experience involves promoting intergenerational collaboration, providing mentorship opportunities, and ensuring that career development is accessible to individuals at different stages of their professional journey.

LGBTQ+ Inclusion

Inclusive leadership extends to LGBTQ+ inclusion. Leaders who actively support and advocate for LGBTQ+ individuals create an environment where everyone feels safe, respected, and valued. LGBTQ+ inclusion involves implementing inclusive policies, fostering awareness, and actively addressing discrimination to ensure that the workplace is welcoming to individuals of all sexual orientations and gender identities.

Disabilities and Inclusion

Leadership that embraces diversity also includes individuals with disabilities. Leaders who create an inclusive environment for individuals with disabilities contribute to a workplace where everyone can thrive. Disabilities and inclusion involve providing reasonable accommodations, fostering accessibility, and promoting an attitude of respect and understanding toward individuals with diverse abilities.

Socioeconomic Diversity

Socioeconomic diversity reflects the inclusion of individuals from various socioeconomic backgrounds. Leaders who actively promote socioeconomic diversity create opportunities for individuals from different economic circumstances to contribute their talents. Socioeconomic diversity involves addressing barriers to entry, providing fair compensation, and ensuring that individuals from all economic backgrounds have access to professional development opportunities.

Intersectionality in Diversity

Intersectionality recognizes that individuals may belong to multiple identity groups, and their experiences are shaped by the intersection of these identities. Leaders who understand and address intersectionality create a more nuanced approach to diversity and inclusion. Intersectionality involves recognizing that individuals may face unique challenges based on the combination of their identities and actively working to create an inclusive environment that addresses the specific needs and experiences of individuals with intersecting identities.

Data-Driven Diversity Initiatives

Effective diversity initiatives are data-driven. Leaders who analyze and monitor diversity metrics, such as representation, pay equity, and employee satisfaction, can identify areas for improvement and track progress over time. Data-driven diversity initiatives involve using analytics to inform decision-making, set benchmarks, and ensure that diversity efforts are impactful and sustainable.

Diversity Training and Education

Promoting diversity requires ongoing training and education. Leaders who invest in diversity training programs create a workforce that is knowledgeable about the importance of diversity, equity, and inclusion. Diversity training and education involve raising awareness about unconscious biases, promoting cultural competency, and fostering an environment where individuals actively engage in learning about different perspectives.

Allyship and Advocacy

Leaders play a crucial role in fostering allyship and advocacy. Leaders who actively champion diversity act as allies for underrepresented individuals, advocate for inclusive policies, and use their positions to amplify diverse voices. Allyship and advocacy involve creating a culture where individuals feel supported, represented, and empowered to bring their authentic selves to the workplace.

Employee Resource Groups (ERGs)

Employee Resource Groups are valuable platforms for fostering diversity and inclusion. Leaders who support and encourage the formation of ERGs create spaces where employees with shared identities or interests can connect, collaborate, and contribute to a more inclusive workplace. ERGs involve providing resources, recognition, and opportunities for employees to engage in initiatives that promote diversity.

Supplier Diversity

Diversity extends beyond internal practices to supplier relationships. Leaders who prioritize supplier diversity actively seek out and support businesses owned by individuals from underrepresented groups. Supplier diversity involves ensuring that the organization's supply chain reflects a commitment to inclusivity, creating economic opportunities for diverse entrepreneurs, and contributing to a more equitable business ecosystem.

Measuring Inclusion and Belonging

Inclusion is an integral part of diversity. Leaders who measure and prioritize inclusion and belonging ensure that employees not only represent diverse backgrounds but also feel valued, respected, and included in the workplace. Measuring inclusion and belonging involves seeking feedback, conducting surveys, and implementing initiatives that contribute to a culture where every individual feels a sense of belonging.

Diverse Representation in Media and Branding

Leaders who champion diversity also consider representation in media and branding. Promoting diverse images, stories, and voices in organizational communications reflects a commitment to inclusivity. Diverse representation in media and branding involves showcasing a variety of perspectives, backgrounds, and experiences, fostering an external image that aligns with the organization's dedication to diversity.

Building a Culture of Belonging

Diversity efforts culminate in the creation of a culture of belonging. Leaders who actively foster a culture where every individual feels valued, respected, and an integral part of the organization contribute to a workplace where diversity thrives. Building a culture of belonging involves addressing systemic barriers, fostering open communication, and actively promoting an environment where diversity is not just embraced but celebrated.

Addressing Microaggressions

Leadership that prioritizes diversity addresses microaggressions. Leaders who recognize and actively work to eliminate microaggressions create a workplace where individuals feel safe and supported. Addressing microaggressions involves providing education, fostering open communication, and implementing policies that promote a culture of respect and understanding.

Leadership Accountability

Leadership accountability is essential for the success of diversity initiatives. Leaders who hold themselves and their teams accountable for promoting diversity, equity, and inclusion ensure that these values are embedded in the organizational culture. Leadership accountability involves setting clear expectations, regularly evaluating progress, and actively addressing challenges to create an environment where diversity is a shared responsibility.

Continuous Evolution of Diversity Initiatives

Diversity initiatives require continuous evolution. Leaders who regularly assess the effectiveness of diversity programs, gather feedback, and adapt strategies ensure that the organization remains at the forefront of inclusive practices. The continuous evolution of diversity initiatives involves staying informed about emerging best practices, industry standards, and societal changes that may impact diversity and inclusion efforts.

Conclusion

As we delve into the profound impact of Diversity in 'The Speed of Leadership,' let us recognize that it's not just about meeting quotas or fulfilling checkboxes. Diversity is the driving force that propels organizations toward innovation, resilience, and enduring success. In embracing the rich tapestry of human experiences, leaders pave the way for a future where every individual contributes their unique strengths to create a workplace that not only reflects the diversity of the world but actively celebrates it.

Chapter 10: Empathy

"Learning to stand in somebody else's shoes, to see through their eyes, that's how peace begins. And it's up to you to make that happen. Empathy is a quality of character that can change the world."

- Barack Obama

Our focus deepens into the transformative power of Empathy. It's not just a soft skill; it's the cornerstone that fosters understanding, strengthens relationships, and fuels a culture of compassion.

The Essence of Empathy

Empathy transcends sympathy; it's the ability to understand and share the feelings of others. Exceptional leaders recognize that empathy is not a sign of weakness but a profound strength that builds trust, enhances communication, and nurtures a sense of belonging. The essence of empathy lies in cultivating a genuine connection with the emotions and experiences of those within the organization.

Empathetic Leadership

Empathetic leadership involves placing oneself in the shoes of others, seeking to understand their perspectives, and responding with compassion. Leaders who embody empathetic leadership create an environment where individuals feel seen, heard, and valued. Empathetic leadership involves recognizing the unique challenges and triumphs of team members and actively demonstrating a commitment to their well-being.

Active Listening

Empathy begins with active listening. Leaders who practice active listening demonstrate a genuine interest in the thoughts and feelings of others. Active listening involves giving full attention, suspending judgment, and providing feedback that reflects a deep understanding of the speaker's perspective. It's a foundational element that establishes trust and opens the channels for meaningful communication.

Understanding Diverse Perspectives

Empathy extends to understanding diverse perspectives. Leaders who actively seek to comprehend the experiences, backgrounds, and values of individuals from different walks of life foster an inclusive and empathetic culture. Understanding diverse perspectives involves recognizing that each person brings a unique viewpoint to the table, enriching the collective tapestry of the organization.

Emotional Intelligence

Empathy is a cornerstone of emotional intelligence. Leaders who cultivate emotional intelligence recognize and manage their own emotions while also being attuned to the emotions of others. Emotional intelligence involves empathetic responses, effective communication, and the ability to navigate complex interpersonal dynamics with grace and authenticity.

Compassionate Decision-Making

Empathy influences decision-making. Leaders who consider the emotional impact of decisions on individuals and the broader team demonstrate compassionate decision-making. Compassionate decision-making involves balancing the needs of the organization with an understanding of how choices may affect the well-being and morale of those involved.

Support in Times of Challenge

True empathy shines in times of challenge. Leaders who offer support, understanding, and a listening ear during difficult periods foster a culture of resilience and trust. Support in times of challenge involves recognizing when team members are facing personal or professional hardships and providing encouragement, resources, or flexibility to navigate through the difficulties.

Acknowledging Successes and Milestones

Empathy includes celebrating successes. Leaders who take the time to acknowledge and celebrate individual and team achievements create a culture where accomplishments are valued. Acknowledging successes involves expressing genuine joy, recognizing the efforts that led to success, and reinforcing a sense of pride and accomplishment within the team.

Recognizing Individual Needs

Empathy involves recognizing and responding to the individual needs of team members. Leaders who understand that individuals have unique challenges, preferences, and aspirations can tailor their leadership approach to provide the necessary support. Recognizing individual needs involves creating a workplace where flexibility, inclusivity, and personalization are valued.

Cultivating a Culture of Care

Empathy contributes to a culture of care. Leaders who actively demonstrate care for the well-being of their team members foster an environment where individuals feel valued beyond their professional contributions. Cultivating a culture of care involves promoting work-life balance, mental health awareness, and initiatives that prioritize the holistic well-being of employees.

Empathy in Communication

Effective communication is imbued with empathy. Leaders who communicate with empathy consider the emotional impact of their words, tone, and delivery. Empathy in communication involves acknowledging the feelings of others, expressing understanding, and fostering an open dialogue where individuals feel comfortable sharing their thoughts and concerns.

Conflict Resolution with Empathy

Empathy plays a pivotal role in conflict resolution. Leaders who approach conflicts with empathy seek to understand the underlying emotions and perspectives of those involved. Conflict resolution with empathy involves facilitating open communication, finding common ground, and working collaboratively to reach resolutions that consider the well-being of all parties.

Building Trust through Empathy

Empathy is a foundation for building trust. Leaders who consistently demonstrate empathy create a trusting environment where individuals feel confident in sharing their challenges, ideas, and aspirations. Building trust through empathy involves being authentic, reliable, and responsive to the needs of the team, establishing a strong foundation for collaboration and shared success.

Mentorship and Empathy

Empathy enhances the mentorship relationship. Leaders who approach mentorship with empathy understand the unique developmental needs, goals, and challenges of their mentees. Mentorship and empathy involve providing guidance, support, and a listening ear, creating a mentorship dynamic that fosters both professional and personal growth.

Balancing Accountability and Empathy

Leadership requires a balance between accountability and empathy. Leaders who hold individuals accountable for their responsibilities while demonstrating empathy create a culture of responsibility and support. Balancing accountability and empathy involves setting clear expectations, providing constructive feedback, and acknowledging the individual circumstances that may impact performance.

Empathy in Organizational Change

Empathy is a guiding force in organizational change. Leaders who approach change with empathy acknowledge the emotions and concerns of individuals affected by the change. Empathy in organizational change involves communicating transparently, providing support mechanisms, and actively addressing the emotional aspects of transitions to create a smoother and more well-received change process.

Self-Reflection and Empathy

Empathy begins with self-reflection. Leaders who engage in self-reflection develop a heightened awareness of their own emotions, biases, and reactions. Self-reflection and empathy involve cultivating a deeper understanding of one's own experiences, which, in turn, enhances the capacity to connect empathetically with the experiences of others.

Empathy as a Cultural Pillar

Empathy becomes a cultural pillar when leaders actively promote and reinforce empathetic behaviors within the organization. Leaders who integrate empathy into the organizational culture create a workplace where individuals instinctively understand the importance of compassion, understanding, and connection.

Ethical Considerations in Empathy

Empathy must be guided by ethical considerations. Leaders ensure that their empathetic actions align with ethical principles, respect the boundaries of others, and contribute positively to the organizational culture. Ethical considerations in empathy involve practicing empathy with integrity, authenticity, and a commitment to promoting the well-being of all individuals.

Sustainable Empathy Practices

Empathy is not a one-time effort; it requires sustainable practices. Leaders who consistently integrate empathy into their leadership style, making it a part of everyday interactions, contribute to a positive and resilient organizational culture. Sustainable empathy practices involve weaving empathy into the fabric of leadership, ensuring its enduring impact on relationships, communication, and the overall well-being of the team.

Conclusion

As we immerse ourselves in the transformative realm of Empathy in 'The Speed of Leadership,' let us recognize its profound influence in shaping not only the professional landscape but the very essence of human connections within the workplace. In a world that often moves swiftly, empathy becomes the guiding light that illuminates the path toward understanding, connection, and a culture where every individual feels valued, supported, and truly seen.

Chapter 11: Risk

"You miss 100% of the shots you don't take."

- Wayne Gretzky - Michael Scott

Risk is not just about avoiding pitfalls; it's about embracing calculated leaps, fostering innovation, and steering the organization toward new horizons.

The Essence of Risk

Risk is not merely the potential for failure; it's the catalyst for growth, innovation, and transformative change. Exceptional leaders understand that avoiding risk altogether is a risk in itself. The essence of risk lies in the willingness to step into the unknown, make bold decisions, and adapt to the evolving landscape of challenges and opportunities.

Calculated Risk-Taking

Effective leadership involves calculated risk-taking. Leaders who assess potential risks, weigh the potential rewards, and make informed decisions based on a thoughtful analysis create an environment where innovation flourishes. Calculated risk-taking involves considering both the short-term and long-term implications of decisions, balancing potential gains with potential losses, and ensuring that risks align with the organization's strategic goals.

Innovation and Risk

Innovation and risk are inseparable partners. Leaders who foster a culture of innovation encourage individuals to explore new ideas, experiment with different approaches, and embrace a mindset that sees challenges as opportunities. Innovation and risk involve creating an environment where individuals feel empowered to contribute inventive solutions and where the fear of failure is transformed into a driving force for progress.

Embracing Uncertainty

Risk involves embracing uncertainty as a natural part of the leadership journey. Leaders who navigate ambiguity with confidence, adaptability, and a strategic mindset position their organizations to thrive in ever-changing environments. Embracing uncertainty involves acknowledging that not all variables can be controlled, and success often requires the flexibility to adjust strategies based on emerging factors.

Risk Communication

Effective risk management includes transparent communication. Leaders who communicate openly about potential risks, the rationale behind decisions, and the steps taken to mitigate challenges build trust within the organization. Risk communication involves providing clear information, fostering a culture where individuals feel comfortable expressing concerns, and creating a collaborative atmosphere where everyone understands their role in managing risks.

Learning from Failure

Risk comes with the possibility of failure, but failure is not the end; it's a learning opportunity. Leaders who view failure as a stepping stone to success create a culture where individuals are not afraid to take risks and learn from their experiences. Learning from failure involves analyzing setbacks, identifying lessons, and incorporating insights into future decision-making and strategies.

Risk Appetite and Tolerance

Leadership involves defining and managing risk appetite and tolerance. Leaders who understand the organization's capacity for risk, set clear parameters for acceptable risk levels, and align risk-taking with overall business objectives establish a framework for responsible decision-making. Risk appetite and tolerance involve creating a balance that encourages innovation while ensuring that risks are within acceptable limits.

Strategic Risk Management

Risk management is a strategic imperative. Leaders who integrate risk management into strategic planning identify potential challenges early, allowing for proactive mitigation strategies. Strategic risk management involves considering risks across different aspects of the organization, including financial, operational, reputational, and regulatory dimensions, and developing comprehensive plans to address potential threats.

Ethical Considerations in Risk

Risk-taking must align with ethical principles. Leaders ensure that the pursuit of opportunities does not compromise the organization's integrity, values, or the well-being of stakeholders. Ethical considerations in risk involve making decisions that prioritize transparency, fairness, and ethical conduct, even in the face of potential gains.

Financial Risk and Stability

Leadership involves balancing financial risk with stability. Leaders who make sound financial decisions, consider potential economic fluctuations, and ensure the organization's fiscal health are better prepared to weather challenges. Financial risk and stability involve prudent financial planning, diversification of financial resources, and strategic investments that align with long-term goals.

Strategic Partnerships and Alliances

Risk can be mitigated through strategic partnerships and alliances. Leaders who identify opportunities for collaboration, build strong alliances, and leverage collective strengths enhance the organization's resilience. Strategic partnerships and alliances involve assessing potential partners, aligning goals, and creating mutually beneficial relationships that contribute to shared success.

Anticipating Industry Trends

Leadership involves anticipating industry trends as part of risk management. Leaders who stay informed about emerging trends, technological advancements, and market shifts are better positioned to identify opportunities and challenges in advance. Anticipating industry trends involves continuous monitoring, engaging in industry networks, and adapting strategies to align with evolving market dynamics.

Crisis Preparedness and Risk

Risk leadership extends to crisis preparedness. Leaders who anticipate potential crises, develop contingency plans, and ensure organizational readiness are more capable of navigating unexpected challenges. Crisis preparedness involves scenario planning, establishing crisis response teams, and conducting regular drills to ensure that the organization can respond effectively in times of crisis.

Regulatory Compliance and Risk

Leadership requires a commitment to regulatory compliance. Leaders who understand and navigate regulatory requirements effectively mitigate legal and reputational risks. Regulatory compliance and risk involve staying abreast of relevant laws, engaging legal counsel when needed, and implementing processes that ensure the organization operates within legal and ethical boundaries.

Cybersecurity Risk Management

In the digital age, cybersecurity is a critical aspect of risk management. Leaders who prioritize cybersecurity measures protect the organization from potential threats to data, privacy, and operational continuity. Cybersecurity risk management involves implementing robust security protocols, educating employees about cyber threats, and continuously adapting measures to address evolving cyber risks.

Crisis Leadership and Risk Communication

Effective crisis leadership includes transparent risk communication. Leaders who communicate clearly during crises, provide accurate information, and convey a sense of control contribute to maintaining trust in the organization. Crisis leadership and risk communication involve acknowledging challenges, offering solutions, and demonstrating resilience in the face of adversity.

Environmental, Social, and Governance (ESG) Risks

Leadership encompasses addressing environmental, social, and governance (ESG) risks. Leaders who consider the impact of organizational activities on the environment, engage with social responsibility, and maintain strong governance practices enhance the organization's sustainability. ESG risk management involves aligning business practices with ethical, environmental, and social considerations to create a positive impact on the world.

Resilience as a Response to Risk

Leadership involves building organizational resilience as a response to risk. Leaders who cultivate a resilient culture ensure that the organization can adapt to challenges, recover from setbacks, and thrive in the face of adversity. Resilience as a response to risk involves fostering a mindset of adaptability, providing resources for recovery, and maintaining a positive outlook during challenging times.

Sustainable Risk Management Practices

Risk management is an ongoing process that requires sustainable practices. Leaders who consistently integrate risk management into decision-making, regularly assess risk landscapes, and adapt strategies to changing circumstances contribute to the long-term success of the organization. Sustainable risk management practices involve weaving risk considerations into the fabric of leadership, ensuring its enduring impact on the organization's ability to navigate uncertainties.

Conclusion

As we navigate the intricate dance of Risk in 'The Speed of Leadership,' let us recognize that risk-taking is not a leap into the unknown but a deliberate and strategic movement toward innovation and growth. In a world where change is constant, embracing risk becomes not only a necessity but a skill that propels leaders and organizations toward new horizons, unlocking untapped potential and shaping a future marked by resilience and success.

Chapter 12: Simplicity

"Simple can be harder than complex: You have to work hard to get your thinking clean to make it simple. But it's worth it in the end because once you get there, you can move mountains."

- Steve Jobs

Simplicity is about distilling the essence, eliminating unnecessary layers, and fostering a culture where clarity is the guiding light.

The Essence of Simplicity

Simplicity is not a reduction of depth; it's the art of presenting complexity in a clear and accessible manner. Exceptional leaders recognize that simplicity is not the absence of sophistication but the elevation of essential elements. The essence of simplicity lies in fostering an environment where communication is clear, processes are streamlined, and the focus is on what truly matters.

Clarity in Communication

Effective leadership involves clarity in communication. Leaders who communicate with simplicity convey messages in a straightforward manner, ensuring that information is easily understood by all stakeholders. Clarity in communication involves avoiding unnecessary jargon, providing context when needed, and using language that resonates with the intended audience.

Streamlining Processes

Simplicity extends to streamlining processes for efficiency. Leaders who identify and eliminate unnecessary steps, bureaucracy, and red tape create an environment where teams can operate with agility. Streamlining processes involves evaluating workflows, identifying bottlenecks, and implementing changes that enhance efficiency without compromising quality.

Focused Decision-Making

Leadership requires focused decision-making. Leaders who prioritize essential factors, avoid unnecessary complexity in decision processes, and make choices with a clear understanding of priorities contribute to effective and swift decision-making. Focused decision-making involves aligning choices with organizational goals, considering the most critical factors, and avoiding unnecessary complications.

Prioritizing Key Objectives

Simplicity involves prioritizing key objectives. Leaders who identify and emphasize the most critical goals create a focused and motivated team. Prioritizing key objectives involves aligning team efforts with overarching strategic priorities, ensuring that energy and resources are directed toward the most impactful initiatives.

Eliminating Unnecessary Complexity

Leadership requires the elimination of unnecessary complexity. Leaders who recognize and simplify convoluted systems, structures, or processes create an environment where individuals can navigate challenges more efficiently. Eliminating unnecessary complexity involves regularly evaluating existing frameworks, questioning the relevance of intricate structures, and making adjustments to enhance simplicity without compromising effectiveness.

Agile Adaptation

Simplicity includes agile adaptation to change. Leaders who foster an environment where teams can quickly adapt to evolving circumstances contribute to organizational resilience. Agile adaptation involves embracing a flexible mindset, encouraging innovation, and removing obstacles that hinder the ability to respond swiftly to change.

Clear Goal Communication

Leadership involves clear goal communication. Leaders who articulate organizational goals in a simple, understandable manner inspire alignment and engagement. Clear goal communication involves expressing objectives in concise language, ensuring that every team member understands their role in achieving those goals, and fostering a shared sense of purpose.

Empowering Teams with Clarity

Simplicity empowers teams with clarity. Leaders who provide clear direction, articulate expectations, and eliminate ambiguity create a workspace where individuals can perform at their best. Empowering teams with clarity involves setting clear goals, communicating expectations transparently, and providing the necessary resources for teams to excel.

Communication Channels

Leadership requires simplicity in communication channels. Leaders who establish straightforward and effective communication channels enhance collaboration and information flow.

Communication channels involve selecting tools and platforms that facilitate clear and efficient exchanges, ensuring that information reaches the right stakeholders in a timely manner.

User-Centric Design

Simplicity extends to user-centric design. Leaders who prioritize user experience in products, services, and processes create a more positive and effective interaction. User-centric design involves understanding the needs and preferences of end-users, eliminating unnecessary features or complexities, and creating solutions that are intuitive and user-friendly.

Strategic Planning with Clarity

Leadership involves strategic planning with clarity. Leaders who develop clear and concise strategic plans provide a roadmap that guides the organization toward success. Strategic planning with clarity involves distilling complex strategies into actionable steps, ensuring that the entire organization understands the overarching vision, and communicating the strategic direction in a way that resonates with all stakeholders.

Efficient Time Management

Simplicity contributes to efficient time management. Leaders who prioritize tasks, avoid unnecessary meetings or processes, and create a culture of productivity enhance the organization's ability to use time effectively. Efficient time management involves recognizing and addressing time-wasting activities, promoting a focus on high-priority tasks, and fostering a work environment where individuals can maximize their productivity.

Simplifying Communication Channels

Leadership requires simplifying communication channels for accessibility. Leaders who ensure that communication channels are clear, inclusive, and accessible to all team members create an environment where everyone can participate effectively. Simplifying communication channels involves choosing platforms that accommodate diverse communication styles, considering the preferences of team members, and providing avenues for open and transparent dialogue.

Measuring Success with Key Metrics

Simplicity involves measuring success with key metrics. Leaders who focus on a few critical performance indicators create a more manageable and impactful measurement system. Measuring success with key metrics involves identifying the most essential factors that reflect progress toward goals, avoiding data overload, and using metrics that provide actionable insights.

Iterative Improvement

Leadership embraces iterative improvement. Leaders who foster a culture of continuous improvement encourage teams to identify and implement small, incremental changes that contribute to overall efficiency. Iterative improvement involves regularly assessing processes, seeking feedback from team members, and making adjustments that enhance simplicity and effectiveness.

Mindful Delegation

Simplicity in leadership includes mindful delegation. Leaders who delegate tasks with clarity, provide necessary resources, and empower individuals to take ownership contribute to a culture of accountability. Mindful delegation involves matching tasks with team members' strengths, setting clear expectations, and creating a supportive environment where individuals can excel.

Clarity in Crisis Management

Leadership requires clarity in crisis management. Leaders who communicate transparently during crises, provide clear guidance, and focus on essential actions contribute to effective crisis resolution. Clarity in crisis management involves developing robust crisis response plans, ensuring that communication is timely and accurate, and demonstrating confidence and reassurance during challenging times.

Balance in Simplicity

Leadership involves finding the balance in simplicity. Leaders who maintain simplicity while recognizing the need for complexity in certain situations create a nuanced and adaptable leadership style. Balance in simplicity involves understanding when to streamline processes and when to allow for necessary intricacies to achieve specific goals.

Sustainable Simplicity Practices

Simplicity is a practice that requires sustainability. Leaders who consistently integrate simplicity into their leadership style, making it a part of everyday interactions, contribute to a positive and resilient organizational culture. Sustainable simplicity practices involve weaving simplicity into the fabric of leadership, ensuring its enduring impact on communication, decision-making, and overall organizational effectiveness.

Conclusion

Let us recognize simplicity's profound influence in creating a workplace where clarity, efficiency, and focus converge. In a world that often bombards us with complexities, simplicity becomes the guiding principle that allows leaders and organizations to move with grace, purpose, and a clear vision toward enduring success.

Chapter 13: Honesty

"Honesty is the cornerstone of all success, without which confidence and ability to perform shall cease to exist."

- Mary Kay Ash

Our focus deepens into the transformative power of Honesty. It's not just about truth-telling; it's about creating a culture where openness is the cornerstone, and integrity is the compass guiding every decision.

The Essence of Honesty

Honesty is not merely a policy; it's the foundation upon which trust is built. Exceptional leaders understand that honesty is not just about conveying facts; it's about being true to one's values, principles, and commitments. The essence of honesty lies in fostering an environment where open communication is valued, transparency is the norm, and integrity is upheld.

Transparent Communication

Effective leadership involves transparent communication. Leaders who communicate openly about organizational goals, challenges, and decisions create an environment where trust can flourish. Transparent communication involves sharing information honestly, addressing concerns promptly, and providing context to help team members understand the broader context of decisions.

Integrity as a Guiding Principle

Honesty is intertwined with integrity. Leaders who make decisions aligned with ethical principles, consistently uphold their values, and act with integrity inspire confidence and respect. Integrity as a guiding principle involves being true to one's moral compass, even when faced with difficult choices, and setting an example that encourages ethical behavior throughout the organization.

Openness to Feedback

Leadership requires openness to feedback. Leaders who welcome constructive criticism, actively seek input from team members, and value diverse perspectives create a culture of continuous improvement. Openness to feedback involves recognizing that everyone, regardless of their position, has valuable insights to contribute, and actively seeking opportunities for personal and organizational growth.

Authenticity in Leadership

Honesty is synonymous with authenticity in leadership. Leaders who bring their genuine selves to their roles, admit their mistakes, and express vulnerability when appropriate foster a culture where authenticity is celebrated. Authenticity in leadership involves being true to one's values, sharing personal experiences authentically, and creating a workplace where individuals feel comfortable bringing their whole selves to work.

Trust Building

Honesty is the cornerstone of trust building. Leaders who consistently demonstrate honesty in their actions, decisions, and communication build a foundation of trust that is essential for effective collaboration. Trust building involves being reliable, keeping commitments, and ensuring that team members can depend on the integrity of the leader.

Ethical Decision-Making

Leadership requires ethical decision-making. Leaders who assess situations with honesty, consider the ethical implications of choices, and make decisions aligned with values contribute to a culture of integrity. Ethical decision-making involves weighing the potential impact of choices on all stakeholders, avoiding actions that compromise principles, and ensuring that the organization operates ethically.

Acknowledging Mistakes

Honesty includes acknowledging mistakes. Leaders who take responsibility for errors, learn from missteps, and communicate openly about corrective actions create a culture where continuous improvement is valued. Acknowledging mistakes involves humility, a commitment to learning and growth, and demonstrating that misjudgments are opportunities for improvement.

Setting Realistic Expectations

Leadership involves setting realistic expectations. Leaders who communicate honestly about what can be achieved, establish clear goals, and provide realistic timelines create an environment where individuals can perform at their best. Setting realistic expectations involves considering available resources, potential challenges, and ensuring that goals are both challenging and attainable.

Avoiding Deception

Honesty requires avoiding deception. Leaders who prioritize truthfulness, refrain from misleading or deceptive practices, and communicate information accurately build credibility and trust. Avoiding deception involves choosing words carefully, providing complete and accurate information, and being transparent about the organization's actions and intentions.

Communicating Challenges

Leadership involves communicating challenges openly. Leaders who share information about obstacles, uncertainties, and potential difficulties create a culture where individuals are prepared to address challenges collaboratively. Communicating challenges involves fostering an environment where team members feel comfortable expressing concerns, seeking solutions collectively, and contributing to overcoming obstacles.

Transparency in Decision-Making

Honesty is intertwined with transparency in decision-making. Leaders who involve relevant stakeholders, provide clear rationale behind decisions, and communicate openly about the decision-making process create an environment of trust and understanding. Transparency in decision-making involves sharing information about the factors considered, the decision-making timeline, and the anticipated impact on the organization.

Truthful Performance Feedback

Leadership requires truthful performance feedback. Leaders who provide honest assessments of individuals' strengths, areas for improvement, and overall contributions create a culture of growth and development. Truthful performance feedback involves offering constructive criticism with empathy, recognizing achievements, and guiding individuals toward continuous improvement.

Consistency in Values

Honesty involves consistency in values. Leaders who align their actions with their stated values, ensuring that organizational decisions reflect the principles they advocate, build credibility and trust. Consistency in values involves making choices that are in harmony with the organization's mission, vision, and core beliefs.

Addressing Unethical Behavior

Leadership requires addressing unethical behavior with honesty. Leaders who confront and address unethical conduct promptly, apply consequences consistently, and communicate openly about the importance of ethical behavior reinforce the organization's commitment to integrity. Addressing unethical behavior involves creating a culture where individuals understand the consequences of ethical violations and are encouraged to report concerns without fear of retaliation.

Open Dialogue in Conflict

Honesty is essential in open dialogue during conflicts. Leaders who facilitate open and honest communication during conflicts, encourage the expression of diverse viewpoints, and seek resolution collaboratively contribute to a culture of trust and understanding. Open dialogue in conflict involves creating a safe space for individuals to voice concerns, fostering active listening, and guiding teams toward constructive resolutions.

Ethical Considerations in Communication

Leadership requires ethical considerations in communication. Leaders ensure that their communication aligns with ethical standards, respects the privacy and dignity of individuals, and contributes positively to the organizational culture. Ethical considerations in communication involve promoting transparency, avoiding misinformation, and fostering an environment where individuals feel respected and valued.

Whistleblower Protection

Honesty extends to whistleblower protection. Leaders who ensure that individuals who report wrongdoing are protected from retaliation create an environment where ethical concerns can be addressed without fear. Whistleblower protection involves establishing clear policies, communicating the importance of reporting unethical behavior, and taking steps to investigate and address concerns in a fair and transparent manner.

Creating a Speak-Up Culture

Leadership involves creating a speak-up culture. Leaders who actively encourage individuals to voice concerns, provide feedback, and contribute ideas without fear of reprisal foster an environment where openness is valued. Creating a speak-up culture involves acknowledging the importance of diverse perspectives, actively seeking input, and ensuring that individuals feel empowered to express their thoughts.

Trust Repair

Honesty plays a pivotal role in trust repair. Leaders who acknowledge breaches of trust, communicate openly about corrective actions, and demonstrate a commitment to rebuilding trust contribute to a culture of resilience. Trust repair involves transparency, consistency in actions, and a genuine effort to address the root causes of trust issues.

Mentorship with Integrity

Leadership involves mentorship with integrity. Leaders who mentor others with honesty, providing guidance that aligns with ethical principles, create a positive and empowering mentorship dynamic. Mentorship with integrity involves offering advice based on values, encouraging mentees to navigate challenges ethically, and fostering a mentorship relationship built on trust.

Sustainable Honesty Practices

Honesty is not a one-time effort; it requires sustainable practices. Leaders who consistently integrate honesty into their leadership style, making it a part of everyday interactions, contribute to a positive and resilient organizational culture. Sustainable honesty practices involve weaving honesty into the fabric of leadership, ensuring its enduring impact on communication, decision-making, and the overall ethical climate within the organization.

Conclusion

As we delve into the authentic realm of Honesty in 'The Speed of Leadership,' let us recognize its profound influence in shaping not only the professional landscape but the very essence of trust, transparency, and integrity within the workplace. In a world that often tests the strength of ethical foundations, honesty becomes the unwavering compass that guides leaders and organizations toward a future marked by credibility, accountability, and enduring success.

Chapter 14: Inspiration

"If your actions inspire others to dream more, learn more, do more and become more, you are a leader."

- John Quincy Adams

Inspiration is about igniting the flame of passion, fostering a culture where innovation thrives, and lighting the path to collective achievement.

The Essence of Inspiration

Inspiration is not a fleeting emotion; it's the heartbeat of motivation that resonates within individuals and teams. Exceptional leaders understand that inspiration goes beyond words; it's about creating an environment where the collective spirit is elevated, and each member is driven to surpass their potential. The essence of inspiration lies in cultivating a culture where passion, creativity, and purpose converge.

Fostering a Visionary Culture

Leadership involves fostering a visionary culture. Leaders who articulate a compelling vision, aligning it with shared values and aspirations, inspire individuals to work toward a common goal. Fostering a visionary culture involves painting a vivid picture of the future, instilling a sense of purpose, and connecting the vision to the collective mission of the organization.

Leading by Example

Inspiration is intertwined with leading by example. Leaders who embody the values they champion, demonstrate resilience, and exhibit passion for their work inspire others to follow suit. Leading by example involves aligning actions with words, showcasing dedication to shared goals, and creating a standard of excellence that motivates others.

Encouraging Innovation

Leadership requires encouraging innovation. Leaders who create an environment where creative thinking is valued, experimentation is encouraged, and new ideas are welcomed inspire a culture of innovation. Encouraging innovation involves recognizing and rewarding inventive solutions, providing resources for experimentation, and fostering a mindset that embraces change.

Recognition and Appreciation

Inspiration includes recognition and appreciation. Leaders who acknowledge and celebrate individual and team achievements create a positive and motivating work environment. Recognition and appreciation involve expressing gratitude, highlighting contributions, and reinforcing the idea that each member's efforts contribute to the overall success of the organization.

Cultivating a Positive Atmosphere

Leadership involves cultivating a positive atmosphere. Leaders who infuse positivity into the workplace, foster a culture of optimism, and encourage a collaborative and supportive environment inspire individuals to approach challenges with enthusiasm. Cultivating a positive atmosphere involves promoting a can-do attitude, addressing conflicts constructively, and ensuring that individuals feel valued and supported.

Empowering Through Trust

Inspiration is intertwined with empowering through trust. Leaders who delegate responsibilities, trust individuals with autonomy, and provide opportunities for growth inspire confidence and motivation. Empowering through trust involves recognizing and nurturing individuals' strengths, providing opportunities for skill development, and fostering a sense of ownership in each team member.

Communicating a Compelling Narrative

Leadership requires communicating a compelling narrative. Leaders who tell stories that resonate emotionally, articulate the organization's journey, and connect the past, present, and future inspire a shared sense of purpose. Communicating a compelling narrative involves crafting messages that evoke passion, using storytelling to convey values, and creating a narrative that aligns with the aspirations of the team.

Setting Stretch Goals

Inspiration involves setting stretch goals. Leaders who challenge individuals and teams to reach beyond their perceived limits, setting ambitious yet achievable objectives, inspire a culture of continuous improvement. Setting stretch goals involves aligning goals with the organization's vision, providing the necessary resources for success, and fostering a mindset that embraces challenges.

Encouraging Continuous Learning

Leadership requires encouraging continuous learning. Leaders who promote a culture of curiosity, invest in professional development, and recognize the value of ongoing learning inspire individuals to expand their knowledge and skills. Encouraging continuous learning involves providing access to learning opportunities, supporting further education, and creating an environment where individuals feel encouraged to explore new ideas.

Expressing Enthusiasm

Inspiration includes expressing enthusiasm. Leaders who convey genuine excitement about the organization's mission, projects, and goals inspire a contagious energy that motivates others. Expressing enthusiasm involves showcasing passion for the work, expressing optimism about future possibilities, and creating a dynamic and vibrant work environment.

Nurturing a Sense of Belonging

Leadership involves nurturing a sense of belonging. Leaders who create an inclusive environment, foster strong team bonds, and ensure that each member feels valued and connected inspire a sense of belonging. Nurturing a sense of belonging involves promoting diversity and inclusion, addressing concerns promptly, and fostering a culture where every individual's unique contributions are appreciated.

Providing Clear Direction

Inspiration is intertwined with providing clear direction. Leaders who communicate a clear roadmap, define expectations, and offer guidance inspire confidence and clarity. Providing clear direction involves aligning goals with the organization's vision, ensuring that team members understand their roles, and creating a structured framework that supports success.

Mentorship and Guidance

Leadership requires mentorship and guidance. Leaders who invest time in mentoring individuals, offering guidance, and providing support inspire a culture of mentorship and continuous development. Mentorship and guidance involve sharing experiences, offering constructive feedback, and helping individuals navigate their professional journeys.

Creating Opportunities for Impact

Inspiration includes creating opportunities for impact. Leaders who empower individuals to contribute meaningfully, recognize the significance of each role, and provide platforms for showcasing achievements inspire a sense of purpose. Creating opportunities for impact involves aligning tasks with individuals' strengths, acknowledging the value of contributions, and ensuring that each member understands their role in achieving organizational goals.

Adapting to Change with Resilience

Leadership requires adapting to change with resilience. Leaders who embrace change positively, demonstrate adaptability, and guide teams through transitions inspire confidence in uncertain times. Adapting to change with resilience involves communicating openly about changes, addressing concerns empathetically, and fostering a mindset that sees change as an opportunity for growth.

Encouraging Collaboration

Inspiration involves encouraging collaboration. Leaders who foster a collaborative culture, break down silos, and emphasize the collective strength of teamwork inspire a sense of unity. Encouraging collaboration involves promoting open communication, recognizing collaborative efforts, and creating a work environment where individuals feel comfortable sharing ideas.

Celebrating Diversity of Thought

Leadership requires celebrating diversity of thought. Leaders who appreciate different perspectives, encourage open dialogue, and value the richness of diverse ideas inspire innovation and creativity. Celebrating diversity of thought involves creating an inclusive culture where individuals feel comfortable expressing their viewpoints and contributing unique insights.

Respecting Work-Life Balance

Inspiration includes respecting work-life balance. Leaders who promote a healthy balance between work and personal life, recognize the importance of well-being, and support flexible arrangements inspire a culture of holistic success. Respecting work-life balance involves setting realistic expectations, encouraging time off when needed, and fostering an environment where individuals can thrive both professionally and personally.

Sustainable Inspiration Practices

Inspiration is not a momentary spark; it requires sustainable practices. Leaders who consistently integrate inspiration into their leadership style, making it an integral part of organizational culture, contribute to long-term motivation and success. Sustainable inspiration practices involve weaving inspiration into everyday interactions, ensuring that the organization's values and mission continually ignite passion and commitment.

Conclusion

As we immerse ourselves in the uplifting symphony of Inspiration within 'The Speed of Leadership,' let us recognize its transformative power in propelling individuals and teams toward greatness. In a world where the pursuit of excellence is fueled by passion and purpose, inspiration becomes the catalyst that drives leaders and organizations to new heights, fostering a legacy of achievement and collective success.

Chapter 15: Passion

"Success isn't about how much money you make. It's about the difference you make in people's lives."

- Michelle Obama

Cultivating a profound connection to one's work, fostering a culture where dedication thrives, and fueling the journey to unparalleled success, is fueled by passionate leadership.

The Essence of Passion

Passion is not a mere emotion; it's the heartbeat of commitment that resonates within individuals and teams. Exceptional leaders understand that passion is not just about liking what you do; it's about a deep, intrinsic connection that fuels sustained dedication. The essence of passion lies in cultivating an environment where work becomes a source of fulfillment, purpose, and relentless pursuit of excellence.

Finding Intrinsic Motivation

Leadership involves finding intrinsic motivation. Leaders who help individuals connect with the deeper meaning of their work, aligning it with personal values and aspirations, inspire a sense of purpose. Finding intrinsic motivation involves recognizing the unique aspects of each team member, understanding their passions, and fostering an environment where work becomes a meaningful journey.

Aligning Personal Values with Organizational Mission

Passion is intertwined with aligning personal values with the organizational mission. Leaders who communicate a compelling mission, ensuring that it resonates with the values of each team member, inspire a shared sense of purpose. Aligning personal values with the organizational mission involves creating a narrative that reflects shared beliefs, articulating how individual contributions contribute to the broader mission, and fostering a culture where everyone feels connected to the organization's goals.

Encouraging Autonomy and Creativity

Leadership requires encouraging autonomy and creativity. Leaders who provide individuals with the freedom to explore creative solutions, take ownership of their work, and express their unique perspectives inspire a culture of innovation. Encouraging autonomy and creativity involves trusting individuals with responsibilities, promoting a mindset of experimentation, and recognizing that diverse approaches contribute to a vibrant and dynamic work environment.

Celebrating Achievements

Passion includes celebrating achievements. Leaders who acknowledge and celebrate individual and team successes create a positive and motivating work atmosphere. Celebrating achievements involves expressing genuine joy for accomplishments, recognizing the effort behind the success, and reinforcing the idea that each milestone contributes to the collective journey.

Embracing Challenges with Enthusiasm

Leadership involves embracing challenges with enthusiasm. Leaders who foster a positive attitude toward overcoming obstacles, viewing challenges as opportunities for growth, inspire resilience and determination. Embracing challenges with enthusiasm involves communicating a sense of optimism, providing support during difficult times, and reinforcing the belief that challenges are integral to the journey toward success.

Investing in Continuous Learning

Passion requires investing in continuous learning. Leaders who promote a culture of curiosity, value ongoing development, and provide opportunities for learning inspire individuals to expand their knowledge and skills. Investing in continuous learning involves supporting professional development, recognizing the importance of staying updated in a rapidly changing world, and fostering a mindset that sees learning as a lifelong journey.

Creating a Motivating Work Environment

Leadership involves creating a motivating work environment. Leaders who prioritize factors that contribute to a positive workplace—such as clear communication, team collaboration, and a healthy work-life balance—inspire individuals to thrive. Creating a motivating work environment involves addressing factors that impact morale, ensuring fair treatment, and fostering a sense of camaraderie among team members.

Nurturing a Growth Mindset

Passion is intertwined with nurturing a growth mindset. Leaders who encourage a belief in the potential for improvement, foster resilience in the face of setbacks, and inspire a commitment to continuous improvement contribute to a culture of growth. Nurturing a growth mindset involves promoting the idea that abilities can be developed, providing constructive feedback, and creating an environment where individuals are encouraged to take on challenges with a positive and open mindset.

Recognizing and Valuing Contributions

Leadership requires recognizing and valuing contributions. Leaders who acknowledge the unique strengths and efforts of each team member, ensuring that everyone feels appreciated, inspire a sense of belonging. Recognizing and valuing contributions involves expressing gratitude, offering constructive feedback, and creating a culture where individual contributions are acknowledged and celebrated.

Communicating a Compelling Vision

Passion involves communicating a compelling vision. Leaders who articulate an inspiring vision for the future, connecting it to the aspirations of individuals and the organization, inspire a collective journey toward excellence. Communicating a compelling vision involves crafting messages that resonate emotionally, creating a sense of purpose, and ensuring that the vision aligns with the values and goals of the team.

Fostering Collaboration and Team Spirit

Leadership involves fostering collaboration and team spirit. Leaders who create an environment where individuals collaborate seamlessly, support each other, and share a sense of camaraderie inspire a culture of teamwork. Fostering collaboration and team spirit involves promoting open communication, recognizing the strengths of each team member, and creating opportunities for collaborative efforts.

Encouraging Work-Life Integration

Passion includes encouraging work-life integration. Leaders who recognize the importance of a holistic approach to well-being, support flexible arrangements, and promote a healthy work-life balance inspire individuals to thrive both personally and professionally. Encouraging work-life integration involves setting realistic expectations, providing flexibility when needed, and fostering a culture where individuals can achieve success in both aspects of their lives.

Inspiring Through Personal Commitment

Leadership requires inspiring through personal commitment. Leaders who demonstrate unwavering dedication to their work, exhibit a passion for the organization's mission, and lead by example inspire others to invest deeply in their roles. Inspiring through personal commitment involves aligning personal values with organizational goals, showcasing a strong work ethic, and creating a standard of excellence that motivates the entire team.

Embodying Positivity

Passion is intertwined with embodying positivity. Leaders who radiate a positive energy, create an optimistic atmosphere, and approach challenges with a can-do attitude inspire a culture of resilience and optimism. Embodying positivity involves demonstrating optimism in the face of adversity, fostering an environment where negativity is addressed constructively, and encouraging a mindset that sees opportunities in every situation.

Providing Opportunities for Impactful Work

Leadership involves providing opportunities for impactful work. Leaders who empower individuals to take on meaningful projects, ensuring that their contributions have a real impact, inspire a sense of fulfillment and purpose. Providing opportunities for impactful work involves aligning tasks with individuals' strengths and interests, recognizing the potential for positive change, and creating a work environment where everyone feels their work is meaningful.

Building a Supportive Community

Passion includes building a supportive community. Leaders who cultivate a sense of community within the organization, encourage peer support, and foster an environment where individuals feel connected inspire a culture of collaboration and mutual respect. Building a supportive community involves addressing conflicts constructively, promoting inclusivity, and creating a workplace where individuals feel a sense of belonging.

Sustainable Passion Practices

Passion is not a fleeting emotion; it requires sustainable practices. Leaders who consistently integrate passion into their leadership style, making it a part of everyday interactions, contribute to an enduring culture of commitment, enthusiasm, and extraordinary achievement. Sustainable passion practices involve weaving passion into the fabric of leadership, ensuring that the organization's mission and values continue to ignite the flame of dedication and excellence.

Conclusion

As we immerse ourselves in the dynamic force of Passion within 'The Speed of Leadership,' let us recognize its transformative power in propelling individuals and teams toward unparalleled success. In a world where extraordinary achievements are fueled by a profound connection to one's work and an unwavering commitment to excellence, passion becomes the catalyst that propels leaders and organizations to new heights, forging a legacy marked by innovation, perseverance, and collective success.

Conclusion - The Symphony of Leadership

In the culmination of 'The Speed of Leadership,' we find ourselves immersed in the harmonious symphony of timeless principles that transcend the ordinary and elevate individuals to the extraordinary. Each chapter, with its unique melody, has woven a tapestry of wisdom, guiding us on a transformative journey toward becoming not only exceptional leaders but extraordinary human beings.

The Unifying Essence

'The Speed of Leadership' is not merely an acronym; it is a beacon illuminating the path to extraordinary leadership and a purposeful life. As we reflect on the timeless principles encapsulated in Trust, Humility, Ethics, Speed, People, Engagement, Excellence, Drive, Leadership, Encouragement, Adaptability, Diversity, Empathy, Risk, Simplicity, Honesty, Inspiration, and Passion, we discover the unifying essence that binds them together — a commitment to growth, resilience, and the unwavering pursuit of excellence.

Living the Tenets

To live 'The Speed of Leadership' is to embrace the transformative power of Trust, where relationships flourish, and collaboration becomes a force multiplier. It is to embody Humility, recognizing the strength in vulnerability and the wisdom in continuous learning. Ethics guide the journey, ensuring that every step aligns with values, integrity, and a commitment to doing what is right, not just what is expedient.

Speed becomes a dance with time, a strategic rhythm that propels us forward, adapting to change with resilience and embracing the opportunities it brings. People are not just a workforce but a community, a source of strength, creativity, and collective achievement. Engagement is the heartbeat that infuses passion into every endeavor, making work a canvas for innovation and personal fulfillment.

Excellence is not a destination but a continuous journey, a commitment to surpassing expectations and creating a legacy of lasting impact. Drive fuels our ambitions, propelling us through challenges, and Leadership emerges as a symphony conductor, orchestrating the talents of individuals into a harmonious whole. Encouragement becomes the melody that uplifts spirits, fostering a culture of support and celebration.

Adaptability is the key to navigating the complexities of an ever-changing landscape, and Diversity becomes the tapestry that enriches our perspectives, fostering creativity and resilience.

Empathy is the bridge that connects us to others, creating a culture of understanding and compassion. Risk is not a threat but an opportunity, a calculated leap toward growth and innovation.

Simplicity is the elegance that transcends complexity, guiding us to clarity and effective communication. Honesty is the foundation of trust, fostering transparent and authentic connections with others. Inspiration becomes the muse that fuels motivation, creativity, and a shared vision. Passion is the heartbeat that propels us toward extraordinary achievements, transforming work into a source of purpose and fulfillment.

The Extraordinary Leader

By living the tenets of 'The Speed of Leadership,' anyone can ascend to the extraordinary. Leadership is not confined to titles or positions; it is a way of being, a commitment to continuous growth, and a dedication to uplifting others. An extraordinary leader is one who navigates challenges with resilience, embraces diversity with open arms, and inspires a shared sense of purpose.

Such a leader embodies the principles of trust, integrity, and transparency. They lead with humility, recognizing that true strength lies in collaboration and shared success. They are beacons of ethical decision-making, ensuring that every choice reflects a commitment to values and principles.

The extraordinary leader is nimble in the face of change, adapting with grace and guiding their team through uncertainty.

They understand that people are the heart of any endeavor, and genuine engagement is the catalyst for innovation and lasting success. Excellence is not a goal but a standard, and they drive themselves and others toward continuous improvement.

With a relentless passion for their work and a commitment to inspiring those around them, extraordinary leaders create an environment where individuals thrive. They encourage, adapt, and lead with purpose, leaving a lasting impact on their teams and the world.

The Symphony of a Purposeful Life

'The Speed of Leadership' extends beyond the professional realm; it is a guide to living a purposeful and fulfilling life. Trust, humility, ethics, and all the principles within this symphony become the notes that compose a life of meaning and impact. They guide individuals not only in their leadership journeys but in every aspect of their existence.

To live 'The Speed of Leadership' is to navigate life's complexities with grace, build meaningful connections with others, and contribute positively to the world. It is an invitation to be an extraordinary person — someone who leads with integrity, inspires with passion, and lives with a deep sense of purpose.

As we conclude our journey through 'The Speed of Leadership,' let us carry this symphony within us. Let it resonate in our leadership, our relationships, and our lives. May the principles encapsulated in these chapters be the guiding stars that lead us to greatness, and may we, in turn, inspire others to embark on their own extraordinary journeys.

Final Crescendo

In the grand finale of 'The Speed of Leadership,' let the symphony of trust, humility, ethics, speed, people, engagement, excellence, drive, leadership, encouragement, adaptability, diversity, empathy, risk, simplicity, honesty, inspiration, and passion echo in our hearts. For in living these principles, we not only become extraordinary leaders but creators of a symphony that resonates with purpose, impact, and the timeless melody of a life well lived.

The End

www.ingramcontent.com/pod-product-compliance
Lightning Source LLC
Chambersburg PA
CBHW062327290526
45794CB00005B/1930